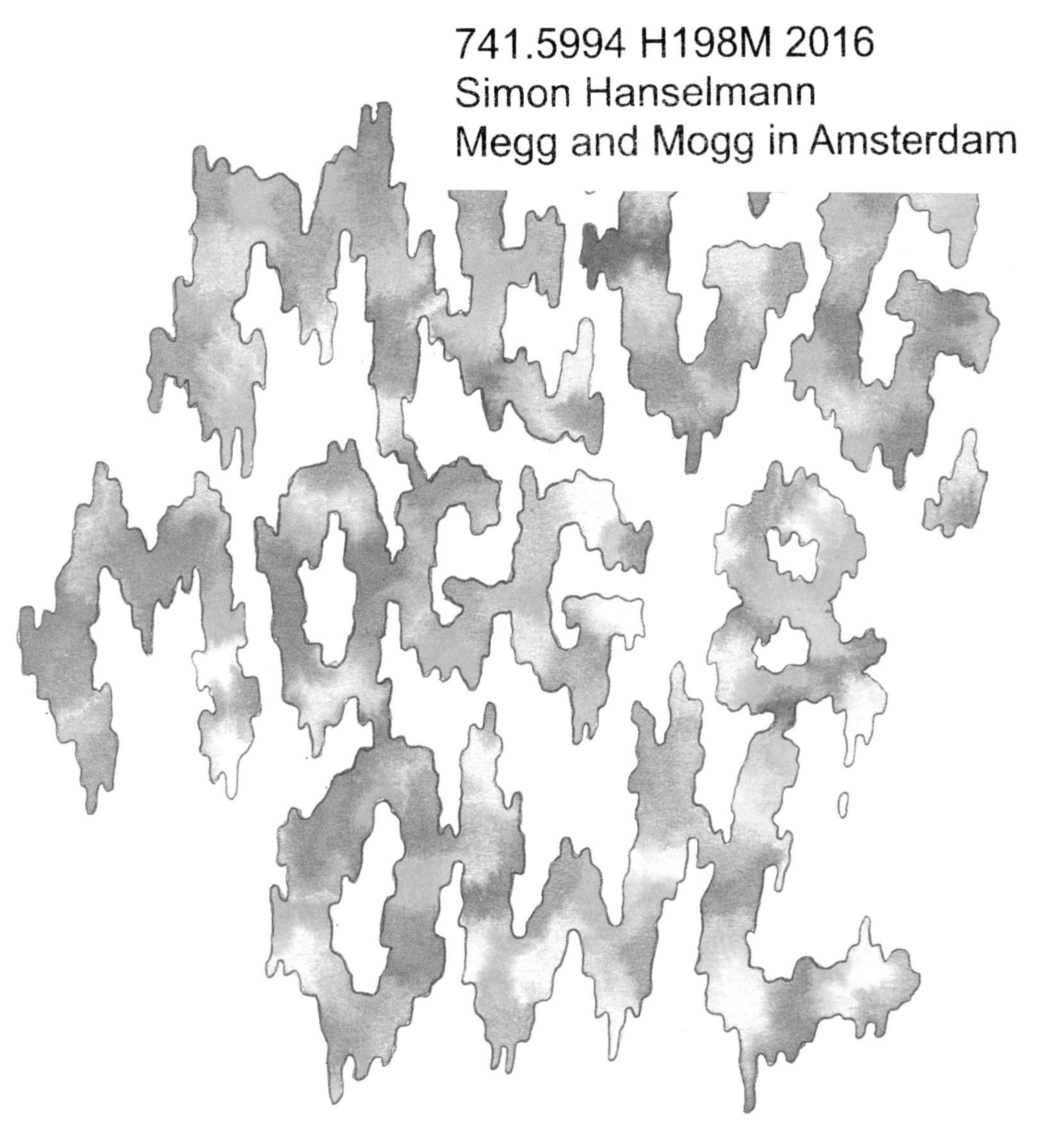

SIMON
HANSELMANN

FANTAGRAPHICS
BOOKS

CONTENTS:

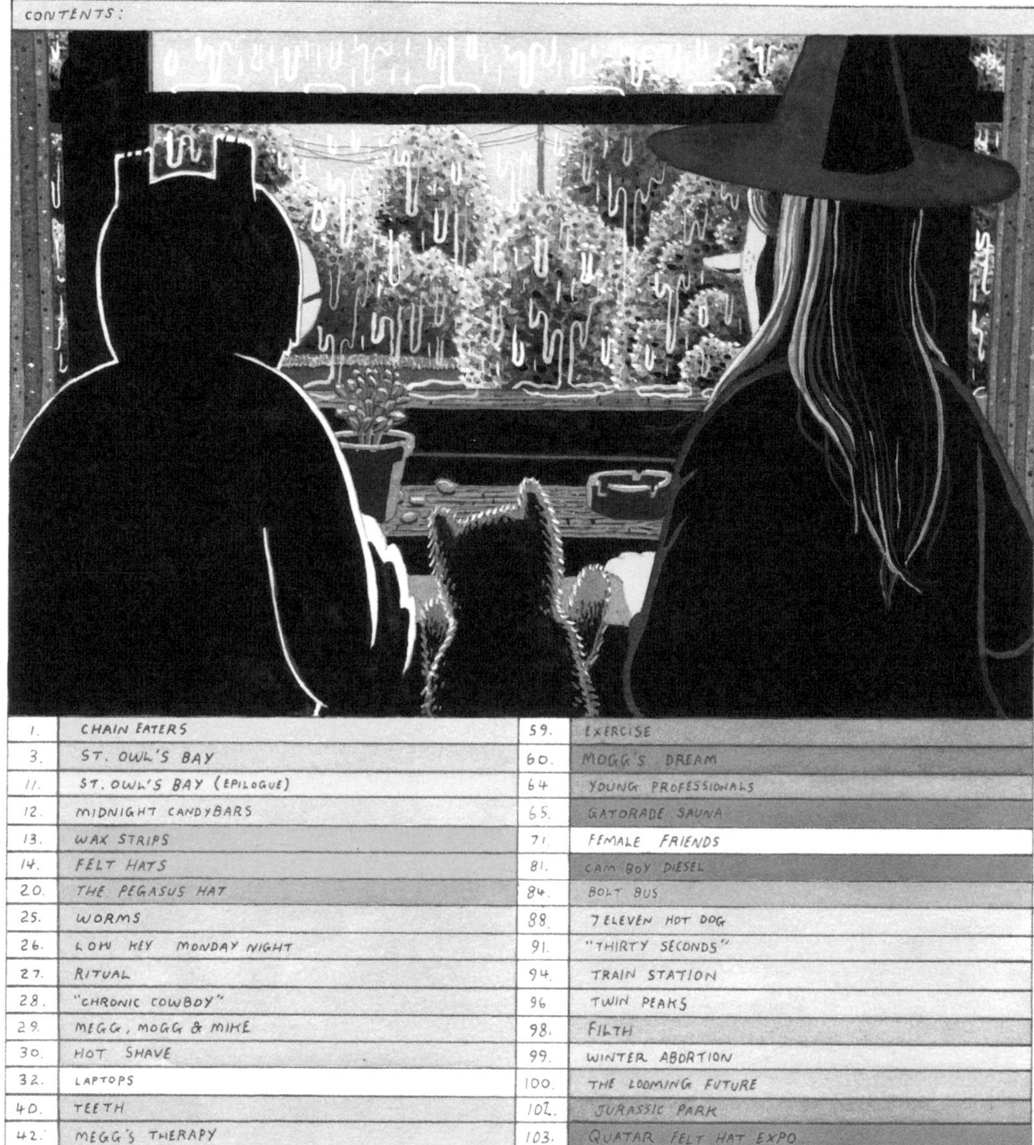

WRITTEN AND ILLUSTRATED BY SIMON HANSELMANN

EDITOR AND ASSOCIATE PUBLISHER: ERIC REYNOLDS
BOOK DESIGN: SIMON HANSELMANN
PRODUCTION: PAUL BARESH
PROMOTION, ETC.: JACQ COHEN
PUBLISHER: GARY GROTH

LIBRARY OF CONGRESS CONTROL NUMBER: 2015959063

ISBN: 978-1-60699-879-3

THIRD PRINTING. SEPTEMBER 2018

FANTAGRAPHICS BOOKS INC. 7563 LAKE CITY WAY NE, SEATTLE, WASHINGTON, USA, 98115

PRINTED IN KOREA.

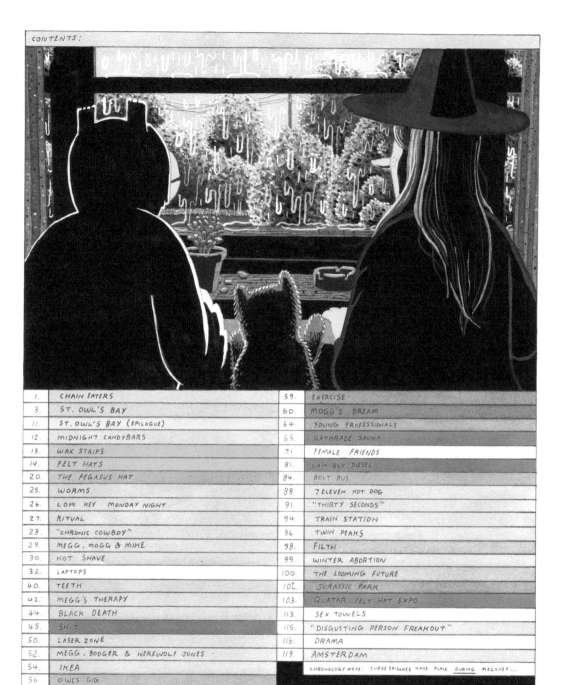

MEGG, MOGG & OWL

GROAN
PIZZA

UGCH.
TOSS
PIZZA

FUCK... MY HEAD'S SPINNING...
ARE YOU OKAY?

YEAH, JUST FEELING A BIT FAINT...
I NEED MORE RED BULL.

SLAM

THAT'S BETTER. NOW I JUST NEED A SMOKE.
OOH! ROLL ME ONE.

I'M ALMOST FINISHED... I'M A LITTLE CHEESE-FILLED BASKETBALL.
GROAN

OH, YEAH?
YEAH.

MMMMMMM.
MMMM

YOU'RE SO GARLICKY
I LOVE IT.

DOUBLE PEPPERONI, DOUBLE GARLIC.

SO FUCKING HOT.

YOU'RE GIVING ME HEART PALPITATIONS!
UGH, WAS THAT THE FRONT DOOR? OWL'S HOME...

HEY, GUYS.
BOOOODOOOOOO

OH, GOD... PIZZAS AGAIN?

IS THAT SEVEN NIGHTS IN A ROW?

... I DON'T KNOW. WHATEVER.

YEAH AND TECHNICALLY IT'S ACTUALLY THE MORNING FOR US, OWL.
GET IT RIGHT.

I'M SERIOUSLY AMAZED THAT YOU GUYS ARE STILL ALIVE...

YOU CAN'T KEEP GETTING UP AT NIGHT AND SLEEPING THROUGH THE DAY AND CHAIN-EATING PIZZAS...

IT'S NOT HEALTHY... I WORRY ABOUT YOU.
GUYS?

ZZZZZZZZZ

HOW CAN YOU SLEEP AFTER DRINKING THIS MUCH RED BULL?...
FUCKING HORRIFYING.

ST. OWL'S BAY
(WET SWORDS)

... I AM PUMPED!!!!!

YEAH ... WE CAN TELL.

OH, MAN. I CANNOT BELIEVE YOU GUYS HAVE NEVER BEEN PROPER CAMPING BEFORE!

I MEAN FUCK!...

FLOATING WORLD
PORTLAND, OR

SIMON HANSELMANN 2013 XOXOXO

YOU'RE GOING TO LOVE IT! THERE'S CAVES AND HOT SPRINGS AND A QUARRY AND THE OLD MINE AND-

ALRIGHT, SETTLE DOWN, FORREST GUMP.
WATCH THE FUCKING ROAD.

SORRY, SORRY! I'M JUST REALLY EXCITED!
THIS IS GOING TO BE THE BEST WEEKEND EV-
FUCKHEAD! THE ROAD!

SCREEECH
HOOONK

LOOK WHERE YOU'RE GOING YOU STUPID BASTARD!
FUCKING OWLS.

SPLAT

!

EW, WHAT IS THAT?

I THINK IT WAS A SHOPPING BAG FULL OF VOMIT

UH-HUH, I USED TO DO A BIT OF "TRUCKING".
WE ALL THREW UP IN BAGS...

AND THREW THEM AT DUMBASS OWLS.

...

HMMMMM...
SEEMS LIKE A BAD OMEN...

NICE GOING, OWL. YOU SCREWED UP THE TRIP ALREADY WITH YOUR STUPID BABBLING.

IDIOT

GODDAMMIT. DRIVE, OWL!
WHAT THE FUCK ARE WE DOING JUST SITTING HERE?

BOOOOOOOOO
BOOOOOOOO
OKAY... WE'RE JUST COMING UP TO IT NOW...
THERE! LOOK AT THAT VIEW!
YEAH... NOT BAD...
LET'S GET DRINKING.
SLAM
DO YOU GUYS WANT TO HELP SET UP THE TENT?
NAH, MAN.
...
UGCH.
WHAT THE FUCK?
WHO PUT MY TENT AWAY WET?!
IT'S ALL FULL OF MOLD
NOT ME.
NOT ME.
PROBABLY NOT ME.
WELL WHERE ARE WE GOING TO SLEEP NOW?!
THIS TENT IS RUINED.
WHO CARES, MAN.
I BROUGHT "THE TACKLE BOX"
I DON'T PLAN ON ANYBODY GETTING MUCH SLEEP.
...
FINE...

WHAT HAVE YOU GOT IN THERE?
EVERYTHING.
WOAH!
FUCK!
DID YOU SEE THAT?
IT'S JUST BATS.
NO, NO... IT WAS BIGGER THAN THAT.
AND IT WAS GLOWING...
HEY, SO WHAT ARE WE DOING?
I THOUGHT WE WERE JUST GETTING DRUNKER UNTIL WE WANT TO GO SWIMMING?
OH, YEAH... OKAY, COOL
CAN WE PUT SOME MUSIC ON UNTIL THEN?
I'M STARTING TO HEAR VOICES.
THAT'S JUST THE NEIGHBOURING CAMPERS.
SOME UGLY FUCKING FAMILY.
BUT YEAH, MUSIC. I'LL GET MY DOCK CRANKING
DAMN, YEAH, THERE WE GO.
"YO"
OH... UH, CAN WE NOT LISTEN TO HIP HOP?
IT'S TOO MUCH... TOO MUCH INFORMATION
I'VE GOT SOME CD'S IN THE CAR...

LOOK, SOME NICE QUIET LO-FI FOLK... OR MAYBE SOME ARTHUR RUSSELL?
DUDE, GET YOUR "COMPACT DISCS" OUTTA MY FACE.
SLAP
"WHOOPS"
"SORRY"
...
OOH, TURN THIS ONE UP.
I LOVE THIS ONE.
ARGH! THEY'RE RAPPING TOO FAST!
WE'RE IN NATURE!
I DON'T WANT TO HEAR ABOUT SOCIAL MEDIA AND LABEL DISPUTES.
UGCH, THESE BEATS ARE AWFUL...
WHY IS IT SO FUCKING AGGRESSIVE?
WOW, OWL. WHAT ELSE DON'T YOU LIKE ABOUT IT?
THE LACK OF SKITS. NOBODY DOES SKITS ANYMORE...
POUR
IT LIGHTENS THE MOOD.
B'OH!
MASH
HAW HAW HAW!
BLAH! WHAT THE FUCK ARE YOU DOING!?
I POURED BOURBON & COKE ON MY PENIS AND MASHED IT INTO YOUR EAR.
NOW QUIT BEING A CRYBABY AND LIGHTEN THE FUCK UP.
SMOKE THIS.
...
WHAT'S IN IT?...
NORTHERN LIGHTS WITH KETAMINE SPRINKLES AND A VALIUM CENTRE.
I CALL IT "THE FUCKSTICK"
OH, SO YOU NAMED IT AFTER YOURSELF...
OOH, BURN!
...
... I'M GOING FOR A WALK...
SIGH

...I WISH MY DAD WAS HERE...
WOAH... DARK...
FWOO!
GLOW WORMS!!
OHHHHHHHH
... THE AIR...
... THE EARTH...
RUSTLE
RUSTLE
... HELLO?

BWAH!!

ARGHHHHH!
KICK
KICK
KICK

AARGGHHHHHH!

TRIP

CRACK
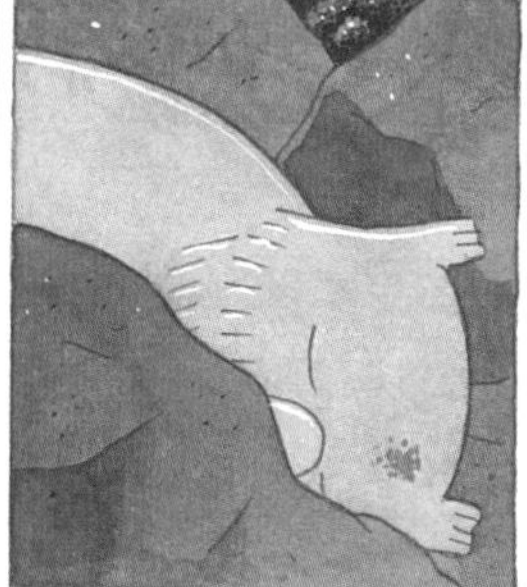

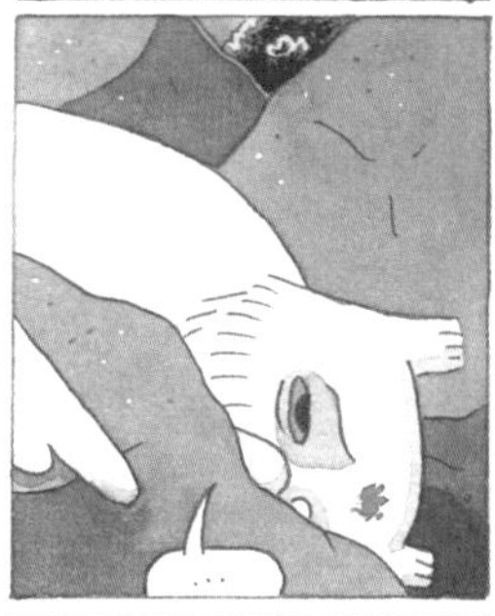
...

GROAN...

OH, HEY, OWL.
...HEY...

WHAT TIME IS IT?

ALMOST MIDDAY...
WE'VE BEEN UP ALL NIGHT!

WERE YOU CREEPING AROUND STEALING FROM OTHER CAMPSITES?
THAT'S WHAT WE DID.

LOOK AT THIS GREAT SHIRT I GOT.
HELLS ANGELS

AND CHECK OUT MY LEATHER BIKINI.

BLUHH
SCRATCH
SCRATCH
IT'S AN ITCHY ONE.

YOU'VE BEEN STEALING THINGS?
...FROM BIKERS?...

HEY, YOU DIDN'T SEE A DOG IN THE WOODS DID YOU, OWL?
... A DOG?...

BRENDA AND ADAM TWO SITES OVER LOST THEIR LITTLE TERRIER...

YEAH, THEY'RE A REALLY SWEET COUPLE AND THEY'RE WORRIED SICK.
DID YOU SEE ANYTHING?...

ARGHHHHHHHH!!
KICK
STOMP
KICK

UHM... I, UH...
...

WE NEED TO LEAVE...
WHAT?
NOW.

... BUT WE'RE HAVING FUN, OWL...
WE HAVE TO GO. FLOOR IT. GO!

FINE. GUH.
YOU'RE SUCH A PARTY POOPER.

... YOU KILLED THAT DOG, DIDN'T YOU, OWL...
WOAH! YOU KILLED RUFFLES?!

I DON'T KNOW...
MAYBE...
THERE WAS SOMETHING IN THE WOODS...

OH, GOD I HOPE IT WASN'T THE DOG...
...

HEY... IT'S THE TRUCKER...
WHAT?!

UGCH!
CREEP.
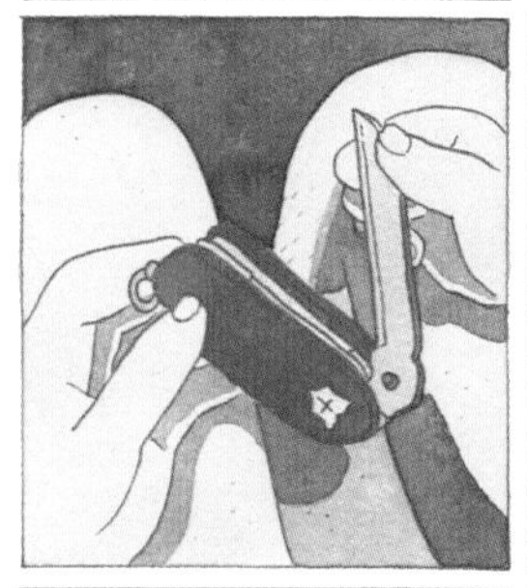

SLASH
PSHHHHHH

LET'S GO TO A ROAD-STOP AND GORGE ON SHIT.

YEAH?...
I COULD USE SOME ROAD-FOOD.

UH-HUH

WE ALL DESERVE A TREAT.

PULL OVER AT THAT McDONALD'S!
I'M PRETTY SURE IT IS...

THAT'S A HALLUCINATION.

NO IT'S NOT.

LOOK, IT'S A DRIVE-THRU. JUST PULL IN.
FOR FUCK'S SAKE.

BLURG, FINE.

SEE? IT'S JUST BUSHES.

OH...

HAHAHAHA!
GROAN

MAN, I'M STILL SO HIGH...

WOAH, THE POLICE DRUG BUS...
POLICE
DRUG SQUAD

NEXT: JAIL

"MEGG,
MOGG
& OWL"

DING DING DING!
YAAAAY!

WHAT'S GOING ON?
IT'S MIDNIGHT, KEEP IT DOWN.

OUR WELFARE MONEY CAME IN!

WE'RE GOING TO THE 7 TO BUY SOME CANDYBARS.
DO YOU... WANNA COME?

OOH, CANDY AT MIDNIGHT?
I DON'T KNOW...

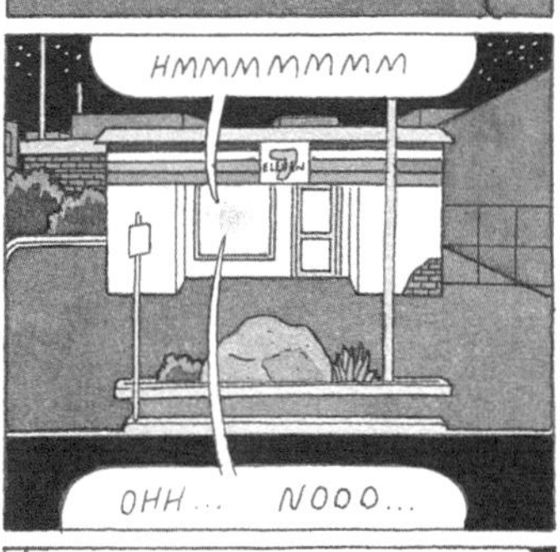
HMMMMMMM
OHH... NOOO...

C'MON, OWL. JUST MAKE A FUCKING DECISION.
OH, I JUST DON'T KNOW.

STOP BEING A DICKHEAD, OWL.
YOU'RE RUINING PAYDAY.

OKAY, FINE, FINE, FINE. I'LL GET A 3 MUSKETEERS.

... I GUESS I'LL BE THE D'ARTAGNAN IN THIS EQUATION.
HA HA.

... GET IT?
Y'KNOW, D'ARTAGNAN...

YEAH. WE GOT IT, OWL.

TOTAL FUCKING BOMB.

REALLY FUCKING LAME, OWL.
UGCH.

"WAX STRIPS"
OW! JUST RIP IT IN ONE MOTION...
FUCK... SORRY
I'M WAY TOO HIGH FOR THIS.
WHY CAN'T YOU DO IT?...
I'M WAY TOO DRUNK...
RIP
ARGGHHHH!
UH-OH
FUUUUUCK!
WHAT HAVE YOU DONE?!
WOAH, GROSS
WHAT DO I DO!?
FUCK!
VEGETABLE OIL?!
IS THAT A THING?...
I, UH-
SPLASH
HAHAHAHAHA!
...
SNORT
WHAT'S GOING ON?!
MOGG SLASHED UP MY VAGINA.
...
CAN YOU STILL COME TO THE BEACH? I'VE BEEN WAITING FOREVER.
YEAH, I'M FINE.
I, uh JUST PUT SOME OF THIS CELLOPHANE IN MY PANTS...
CRINKLE
LET'S DO IT.
CRINKLE
COOL.
...OH, FUCK.
WHAT?
FUCKING WERE-WOLF JONES.
OH, HEY, WW JONES!
DUDES! I NEED YOUR HELP!
I'VE PULLED A HUGE "THURSTON MOORE" AND I NEED TO HIDE OUT FOR A WHILE...
HOW DO YOU DOUCHEBAGS FEEL ABOUT ME CRASHING IN THE SHED FOR A FEW WEEKS?
!
YEAH, WHATEVER, MAN. COOL.
I CAN'T AFFORD TO PAY RENT.
...
BUT I'VE GOT ALL THIS STALE KETAMINE.
WE SHOULD HAVE A PARTY TONIGHT!
SNIFF
COOL! FUCK THE BEACH.
UH, I'VE GOT TO BE UP EARLY FOR WORK TOMORROW...
PARTY!!

MEGG, MOGG & OWL
"FELT HATS"

OH, HEY, OWL.
♫ HOW WAS YOUR DAY, DEAR ♫

YOU GUYS STILL HAVEN'T CLEANED UP FROM YOUR PARTY?
SIGH

... WHAT THE HELL ARE YOU DOING NOW?

I'M MAKING US ALL FELT HATS.
DON'T WORRY, MOTHER, I PUT NEWSPAPERS DOWN.

ARGH!! THOSE AREN'T NEWSPAPERS!! FUCK!
LIFTED BROW
ARTHUR
THOSE ARE MY "ARTS BROADSHEETS"!

GRRRRRRRR!!!
YOU MORON!!

WHOA... WATCH IT, OWL. THAT'S A HATE SLUR

CALM DOWN, HAVE SOME OF MY KETAMINE.
I'LL DO YOUR HAT!

I DON'T WANT ANY KETAMINE OR HATS! I WANT A CLEAN QUIET HOUSE!
... I WANT SLEEP! I WANT TO WATCH 'Q.I.'!

I WAN-
DING DONG
OOH, I'LL GET IT.

...WHO THE FUCK IS THAT?!
"THE PUPS."

WHAT?
WEREWOLF JONES HAS CUSTODY OF HIS PUPS THIS WEEKEND.

EVERYBODY, THIS IS DIESEL AND JAXON.
NOW, YOU BOYS BE GOOD. DADDY'S MAKING HIS HATS.

CAN I HAVE A BONG, DADDY?
SURE, WHY NOT?
...

DADDY, DADDY, LOOK AT ME...
FIDDLE

THIS IS SERIOUSLY UNCOOL, WEREWOLF JONES! YOU GOTTA GET THESE MONSTERS OUT OF HERE!
DADDY.
AAHH, THEY'RE FINE AFTER A FEW BONGS.

...HOW OLD ARE THESE CHILDREN?!
DADDY.
AND WHAT THE FUCK HAVE YOU DONE TO THEM?!

...THEY HAVE CONFECT-IONARY 5 O'CLOCK SHADOWS...
YOU... YOU CAN'T DO THIS. YOU CAN'T HAVE THEM HERE.

AW, C'MON, MAN! IT'S JUST FOR A WEEK.
F-FUCK
THEY'RE MY LITTLE DAWGS! C'MON MAN, BE COOL.

THEY'LL SETTLE DOWN.
AV
DADDY!
...LOOK, JAXON'S GREENING OUT ALREADY.

ARGGHHHHHH! DADDYYYYYY!
CALM DOWN, DIESEL. DON'T YOU THROW THAT ASHTRAY.

CRACK

!
MNGHBN!

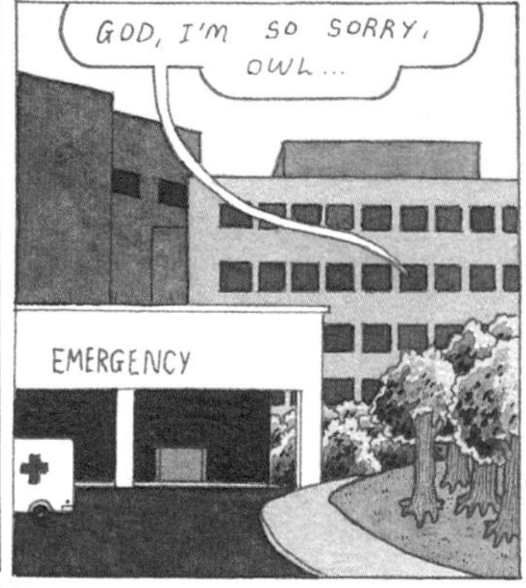
GOD, I'M SO SORRY, OWL...
EMERGENCY

WHAT DO WE SAY, KIDS?
"SORRY".
"SORRY".

UH-HUH.

... THE BOYS AND I FINISHED OFF YOUR HAT FOR YOU.
GO ON, DIESEL.

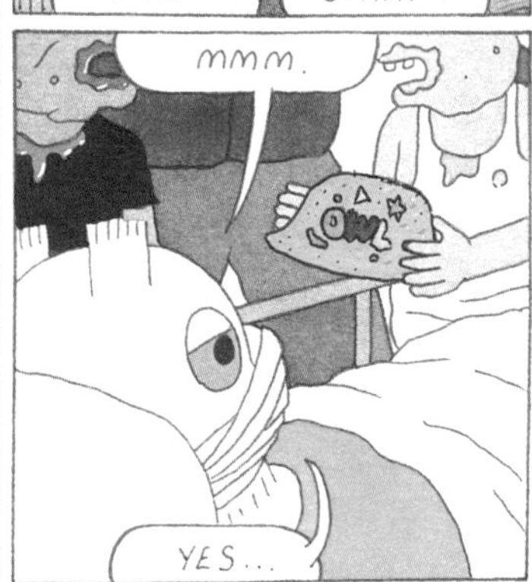
MMM.
OWL
YES...

THAT CAN JUST GO STRAIGHT INTO THE BIN.

HEY, C'MON! THEY WORKED HARD ON THAT!!
DIESEL SAID HE WAS SORRY.

HA HA!

WELL, FRANKLY: HE CAN JUST GO AND FUCK HIMSELF.
YOU ALL CAN.

I'M PRETTY "MORPHED UP" RIGHT NOW AND I JUST WANT TO WATCH WHEEL OF FORTUNE IN THIS CLEAN, QUIET ROOM.

DIESEL, JAXON, YOU'RE REPULSIVE.
YOU OFFEND ME.

FUCK, WHAT AN ASSHOLE...

WHAT DOES "REPULSIVE" MEAN, DADDY?

NOTHING, BOYS, NOTHING! DON'T YOU WORRY ABOUT THAT MEAN OLD OWL!

DADDY'S TAKING EVERYBODY OUT FOR LUNCH!
HOOTERS

THREE LONG ISLANDS AND TWO LIGHT BEERS, THANKS.

I LIKE YOUR HATS.
THANK YOU!

BEAKS

BEAKS
HMMMM...

THE
PELICAN
CLASSIC OLD WORLD STYLING. GREAT FOR BUFFETS WITH EXCELLENT STORAGE CAPABILITIES. 20% OFF THIS MONTH
CODE: 98721672

THE
KIWI
LONG, PLIABLE AND SENSITIVE TO THE TOUCH. PERFECT FOR THE YOUNG URBAN PROFESSIONAL.
CODE: 93621298

BEAKS 6

THE
EAGLE
HEAVY AND HARD FOR THE RISK TAKING ADVENTURER. HOOKED FOR ADDED PIZAZZ.
CODE: 93261762

THE
MALLARD
DASHING BLACK-TIP CLASSIC FOR THE MODERN ALPHA-MALE. ALWAYS A HIT AT PARTIES AND FORMAL SOIREES ALIKE.
CODE: 92613726

7 BEAKS

ONE WEEK LATER...

THANKS, JIMMY.

NO WORRIES, MAN. GOOD LUCK WITH THE NEW BEAK.

LOOKIN' GOOD!

YEAH?

YEAH, BRO', YOU GONNA GET SO MUCH PUSSY IN THE CLUBS.

OKAY... THAT'S A LITTLE CRASS, JIMMY.

BUT *YEAH!*

THANK YOU!

PEEP

HE'S HOME!

OWL!
WOO!

OOH, LOOK AT THAT SEXY NEW BEAK!

UH-HUH. THOSE LITTLE MONSTERS AREN'T STILL HERE ARE THEY?

UHHH...
WELCOME HOME, OWL

RARGHHHH!
HEY, HEY! CALM DOWN!

TOSS!

CRACK!

WHUBUW?!
WHAB DA FBUCG?!

FUCK! I'M SORRY, OWL...
WELCOME HOME, OWL
... I BLAME THE SCHOOL SYSTEM.

"MEGG, MOGG & OWL"

MOTHER FUCKER!

...

WHERE THE HELL DO I FIND THE FUCKING PEGASUS HAT?!

I THINK IT'S IN THE TOWN WITH ALL THE TALKING STONES...

NO. IT'S NOT. I'VE BEEN THERE.
FUCK YOU.

...

SO UH, HAVE YOU LOOKED FOR ANY JOBS, WEREWOLF JONES?

ARGH! GET OFF MY DICK, DAD!

I'LL FIND SOMETHING EVENTUALLY

RIGHT NOW I JUST NEED TO FIND THIS HAT SO I CAN GET INTO THE EN-CHANTED LAKES DISTRICT...

...
HOW LONG HAVE YOU BEEN ZELDA-ING TODAY?

...MAYBE YOU SHOULD GO OUT?

MAYBE YOU SHOULD GO TO A CLUB WITH OWL?
YOU COULD BOTH LEAVE THE HOUSE...

WELL, NOT THAT. BUT YOU DO HAVE TO GET BACK TO REAL LIFE, WW.

YOU CANNOT KEEP LYING HERE ALL DAY TRAIPSING THROUGH DIGITAL DUNGEONS.

...
I WANT TO WATCH A FUCKING DVD.

... I HAVEN'T WANTED TO SAY ANYTHING...
BUT THIS ISN'T MY WEED...

THIS IS BROCCOLI COVERED IN BUG SPRAY...

OH MY GOD!!

ARE YOU FUCKING ACCUSING ME OF STEALING YOUR DRUGS?!

FUCK YOU!!

HEY! CALM DOWN.

YOU HAVE BEEN STEALING SHIT!
AND YOU'VE BEEN PLAYING ZELDA WAY TOO MUCH.

WHATEVER, MAN! WHAT DO YOU KNOW? YOU CAN'T EVEN PLAY ZELDA'S.

I-I CAN KIND OF OPERATE IT...

UGCH. PUT YOUR PENIS AWAY, WW.

NO!

FLOP

JIGGLE

ALRIGHT, THAT'S IT.

YOU'VE OVERSTAYED YOUR WELCOME...
GIVE ME THE CONTROLLER.

NO! I WON'T GO BACK!
I'M NOT GOING BACK!

GIVE IT TO ME.

SMACK

JUST BACK THE FUCK OFF.

I'M PLAYING FOR A FEW MORE HOURS.
THEN I'M GOING TO KILL MYSELF...

AS SOON AS I FIND THE HAT...

MEGG, MOGG & OWL

IS THE DOWNLOAD DONE?
IT'S BACK UP TO... ONE HUNDRED HOURS...

AAARRGGGHHHH!

OH MY GOD!

THERE'S A GIANT WORM IN THE TOILET!

ONE OF YOU HAS FUCKING WORMS!

IT'S NOT ME. IT CAN'T BE...
I HAVEN'T "DONE ANYTHING" FOR LIKE THIRTY-SIX HOURS...

I'VE MOSTLY JUST BEEN SHITTING OUTSIDE... IN THE TREES...

WELL IT'S GOTTA BE ONE OF YOU!

I'M NOT THE ONE WITH THE DISGUSTING DIET AND THE FILTHY SADNESS MATTRESS.
UGCH.

I'M GOING TO GET TO THE BOTTOM OF THIS.
REPULSIVE.

HUFF
STORM

LOW KEY MONDAY NIGHT

MEGG, MOGG & OWL

COUGH COUGH
COUGH COUGH

SPIT

HEY! HAPPY ANNIVERSARY!
COUGH COUGH

SPIT

EW!
ARE YOU DOING YOUR HORRIBLE PHLEGM DRINKING THING?

UH- HUH.

IT'S NOT "HORRIBLE". IT'S ROMANTIC.

"TO ROMANCE"!
SWAP
CLINK

SLURP
GULP

I GOT YOU A MILKSHAKE MAKER.
I'M GOING TO GO THROW UP.

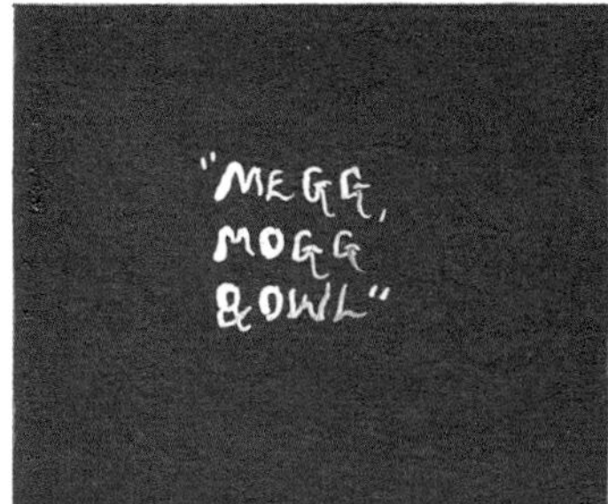
"MEGG,
MOGG
&OWL"

WHAT ABOUT NOW?...
NO. NOW IT'S AT ONE HUNDRED AND THIRTY HOURS...

HEY, UH, GUYS...

I HAD A REALLY HARD DAY TODAY...
DO YOU THINK I COULD ROLL A SMALL JOINT?

OOOOOOOHH...

MMMMMMMM...

WE'RE KIND OF ALMOST OUT...

HOW ABOUT YOU CALL FOR MORE.

MOOOAANNNN
REALLY? BUT IT'S SO AWKWARD... I DON'T LIKE IT.

WELL, THAT'S WHAT'S HAPPENING.
JUST BE CASUAL. DON'T BE SUPER OBVIOUS...

... FINE...
IT'S RINGING...

HELLO? YES, UH, IT'S ME... OWL...
THE... "CHRONIC COWBOY"...

I WAS THINKING OF MOSEYING DOWN TO YOUR "DUDE RANCH"...
I NEED A FEW "BALES OF HAY"...

HELLO?
... THEY HUNG UP...

MEGG, MOGG AND MIKE

GURGLE

PUFF

MAN, MIKE, YOU'RE SO GOOD AT HANGING OUT.

ISN'T MIKE REALLY GOOD AT HANGING OUT?

YEAH, HE'S PRETTY GOOD.
... BETTER THAN OWL.

HOW DO YOU DO IT, MIKE?

I DUNNO.

SIP

I'M JUS' HANGIN'...

"HOT SHAVE"

AAARGH! C'MON, HURRY UP! WE NEED TO LEAVE NOW!

UGCH, CALM DOWN.
I JUST NEED A FEW MORE BUCKETS.

MEGG?! I ASKED YOU TO SHAVE YOUR LEGS!

THAT TAKES A LONG FUCKING TIME, OWL.

AND I'M WAY TOO HIGH.

GODAMMIT! I'M PAYING YOU $50 TO PRETEND TO BE MY GIRLFRIEND.

THIS IS A CERTAIN CLASS OF PEOPLE. THE WHO'S WHO OF TELE-MARKETING!

YOU NEED TO SHAVE THOSE THINGS NOW!
OR NO $50.

OH, FOR FUCK'S SAKE.
FINE.

CLICK

CLICK

...
RUB
RUB

THERE. SMOOTH AS A CREEPY BABY.

CLASSY ENOUGH FOR YOU, PROFESSOR PLUM?

I - I GUESS...

YOU'RE LOOKING A LITTLE SHAGGY THERE, MOGG...
REALLY? SHIT, LIGHT ME UP.

WHOOMF

ALRIGHT,

LET'S FUCKING HIT THIS SHIN-DIG! WOO!

MEGG, MOGG & OWL

UGH.
BURN ME IN A DITCH.

...

CLICK

HELLO?

GUYS?

HELLO?

...

CLICK

UGH.

IDIOTS!

THREE FUCKING BURGLARIES IN THE NEIGHBORHOOD THIS WEEK!

YEAH, LET'S JUST LEAVE ALL THE FUCKING DOORS OPEN!

LET'S LEAVE THE WINDOWS OPEN IN THE RAIN WITH OUR LAPTOPS NEXT TO THEM!

...

HIDE

...THIS'LL SHOW THEM...

CLICK

WELCOME BACK TO ANTIQUES ROADSHOW.
OOH, WE HAVE A LOVELY BAROQUE NAPKIN HOLDER HERE.

OOH!

SIP

UGH. THIS RAIN CAN SUCK MY DICK.

FUCKING STUPID OUTSIDE WORLD.

MY FUR'S SMELLING STANKY...
I MIGHT NEED A BLOW-DRYING.

... OH, THANK GOD...
HOOOOME!

GAH, THE DOOR'S LOCKED...
MUST BE FUCKING OWL.

BANG BANG BANG
OWL!

OWL, LET US THE FUCK IN, YOU FUCKING IDIOT!

ALRIGHT. CALM DOWN.

WHERE'S YOUR KEY?

I DON'T FUCKING KNOW!
PROBABLY IN MY POCKET!

WE DON'T HAVE TIME FOR KEYS, OWL!
FUCK YOUR KEYS!

MMM, SWEATY CHICKEN!
FINGER LICKIN'!

MMMM, THIS SKIN'S SO GREASY AND WET WITH SPICE.

HEY... WHERE'S MY LAPTOP?

WHA... WHERE'S MY LAPTOP?
WHAT THE FUCK?!

OWL, DID YOU MOVE OUR FUCKING LAPTOPS?

WHAT?
NO.

I ONLY GOT BACK FROM WORK TEN MINUTES AGO...

WHAT THE FUCK!? THEY WERE RIGHT HERE?!

HMMMM.
I HAVE NO IDEA...

WHA- I...
...

GOLLY, DO YOU THINK MAYBE THEY WERE... STOLEN?

ALL THE DOORS WERE OPEN WHEN I GOT HOME...
AND THE WINDOW THERE.

THERE'VE BEEN QUITE A FEW BURGLARIES AROUND RECENTLY...

BURGERLERIES?

HAVEN'T YOU BEEN WATCHING THE LOCAL NEWS?

EW, NO.
THE NEWS IS FOR LOSERS, OWL.

IT'S ALL JUST FAKE BULLSHIT MADE UP BY THE PIGS TO SCAM YOU INTO BEING A PUSSY.

...
BUT WHERE ARE OUR FUCKING LAPTOPS?

INDEED... I THINK MAYBE THEY'VE BEEN STOLEN...

NONONONONONO
THEY MUST JUST BE IN OUR ROOM!

FUCK...

OH GOD
OH GOD
OH GOD

FUCK!!
OH GOD OH GOD OH GOD

THEY'VE BEEN FUCKING STOLEN!
FUUUUUCK!!!

I TOLD YOU GUYS...
YOU CAN'T KEEP LEAVING THINGS UNLOCKED.

THIS WAS BOUND TO HAPPEN.

AAARRGHHH!!

MY FUCKING SELFIES!
MY MUSIC!

MY PORN!
MY MEMOIRS!

SOB

UGCH, SOME DISGUSTING CREEP'S PROBABLY CREAMING HIMSELF OVER MY NUDES.
ARGH, I CAN FEEL IT.

I NEED MY MEMOIRS! MY LIFE!
WHAT DID I DO LAST WEEK?! I CAN'T REMEMBER!

IT'S LIKE I DON'T EVEN EXIST ANYMORE!
WHO AM I?! WHAT AM I DOING?!

HAHAHA!

FUCK, WE GOTTA CALL THE PIGS...
OH MY GOD. SO GROSS.

...

WHAT THE~

GOTCHA.

I'M SORRY I HAD TO SPOOK YOU LIKE THAT...
BUT YOU NEEDED TO BE TAUGHT A LESSON.

I DON'T FEEL SAFE IN THE HOUSE WITH ALL THESE UNLOCKED DOORS.
THIS SHIT NEEDS TO STOP.

RAARGHHH!
SOCK!

SLAP
ARG!

MEGG!? STOP!
WHOOMP
OOF!

DON'T STOP!
GET HIM!

!
CRACK

OHHHHHHHHHH

...
NEVER...

NEVER AGAIN, OWL.

YOU PULL ANYTHING LIKE THAT EVER AGAIN...
I'LL PUT YOU IN THE GROUND.

... GO AND OPEN ALL THE DOORS, MOGG.
YES, MA'AM.

OOH.
8 LIKES ON MY NEW PROFILE PIC.

"MEGG, MOGG BOWL"

DO UH... DO YOU WANT SOME GUM, MEGG?
WHAT? WHY?

DO I HAVE SMELLY BREATH?
...

IT'S TOTALLY STINKING UP THE WHOLE ROOM.
OF COURSE YOU DON'T!

... GIMME THE GUM.

OH, THANK GOD.
CHEW
CHEW
CHEW

AAAARRRGGGHH!
FUCK!

OH MY GOD!!
WHAT?! WHAT?

MY FUCKING TOOTH JUST CRUMBLED AWAY INTO THE GUM!

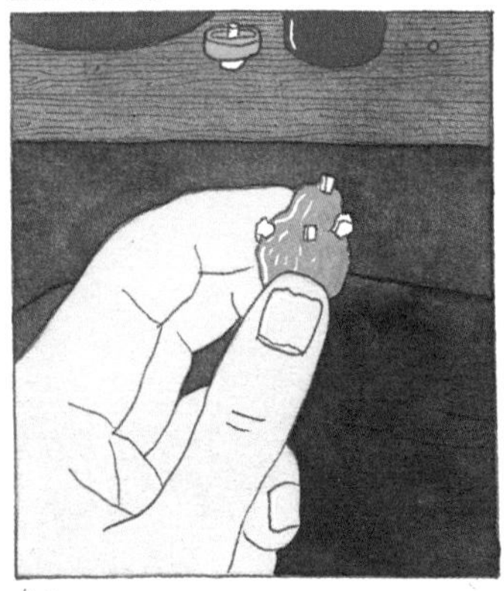

OH, FUCK IT FEELS HORRIBLE!
WHAT DO I DO?! WHAT DO I DO?!

CALM DOWN, IT'S OKAY. I'LL CALL MY DENTIST
AARRRRGHHH!

AND SO:
I WONDER HOW SHE'S DOING?
SHE'S BEEN GONE FOR HOURS.

THANKS FOR ORGANIZING THE APPOINTMENT, OWL
AND LENDING US THE MONEY.

THAT WAS REALLY NICE OF YOU.
HEY... C'MON.

WOOOOOOOOOO!
OH, SHE'S BACK!

HEEEEE-EEEEEY!
GIN
BREDOOOWWW!

CHECK OUT MY NEW FUCKING DRESS

SLAM
GIN

WHAT HAPPENED AT THE DENTIST?

BAH! FUCK THAT PIRATE!
MY TEETH ARE FINE.

I GOT US A NINTENDO!
SOME GUY IN THE STREET WAS UNLOADING THEM CHEAP.

WOAH! COOL!

WHA?...
BANANAS?

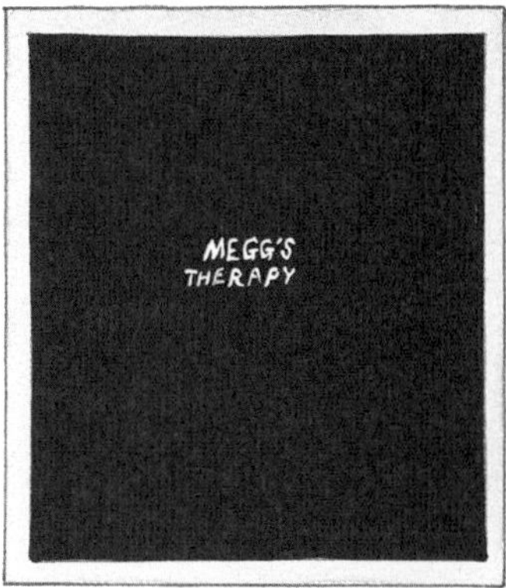
MEGG'S
THERAPY

OH, HEY, MEGG. WHERE ARE YOU OFF TO?

THERAPY.

OH.
...HOW'S IT GOING?

MEH... KIND OF BLAH. I.D.K.

SHE'S A BIT... BOUNDARY CROSSY...

HMMMMMM.

THE BEST PART OF THERAPY IS THE RETAIL THERAPY AFTERWARDS.
HMMMMMM.

UH-HUH. WELL, I GOTTA GO.
HMMMMM...

SORRY I'M SO LATE, MEGG! I GOT DISTRACTED AT THE SALES!
COME IN!

OH MY GOD, YOU LOOK HOT TODAY, MEGG.
DAMN!

...OH, UH... THANKYOU...

YOU REALLY DO REMIND ME OF THIS GIRL I USED TO DATE IN THE LATE EIGHTIES.

...I LOVED HER MORE THAN ANYTHING...

...

YOU LOOK TENSE. I'LL TELL YOU WHAT:
I'VE STARTED DABBLING IN SPIRITUAL MASSAGE.

HERE'S MY ADDRESS. I'M FREE MOST NIGHTS AFTER TEN...
FREE TRIAL. THINK ABOUT IT.

JALD'S
PIZZ

ALD'S
PIZZA

"SPIRITUAL MASSAGE"...
ALD'S

YEAH, RIGHT.
ALD'S

BLACK DEATH

... FUCK.
WHAT?

WEREWOLF JONES IS STUCK WITH HIS KIDS OUT IN HICKSVILLE.
NO WEED UNTIL TOMORROW...

OH, SHIT. WHAT?
BUT THIS IS OUR LAST LITTLE SCRAP-JOINT.

WHAT THE FUCK ARE WE GOING TO DO?

... I'M PRETTY SURE I DROPPED A FEW CRUMBS DOWN HERE LAST WEEK...
HMMMMM

I STUFFED SOME STALKS IN THIS COUCH CRACK LAST MONTH!

... FUCK.
IT'S NOT MUCH.

MAYBE WE SHOULD DREDGE THE BUCKET FOR BLACK DEATH?
OH, GOD...

MAYBE.

THERE'S SOME GOOD STUFF IN THERE.
WE'LL DRY IT IN THE MICROWAVE.

SIGH

LET'S JUST GO TO LIQUOR TOWN.

THIS SUCKS.

FUCKING STUPID WW JONES...
AND HIS STUPID FUCKING UGLY KIDS.

"SHIT"

YEAH, HEY, "W". IT'S "M".

YOU STILL GOT THOSE... "GREEN HATS"?...

COOL, COOL... WE'LL BE OVER IN FIFTEEN.

♫ POOP POOP POOP POOP
♫ BREOW BREOW BREOW BREOW

UGH...

SO MUCH SHIT...
DID WW GET A DOG?

KNOCK
KNOCK
KNOCK

... GODDAMN THAT'S A LOT OF SHIT...

PEEP

OH, HEY GUYS. COME ON IN.

RARGHHHH!!
BWAHHW!!

MNNGHHHGHHM!!
...

MWAAAAHHHHH!!
CALM DOWN, BOYS!

BACK! BACK!
MRAWGHHBWN!

YAH!
YAH!

GET IN THERE!
YOU STAY IN THERE!

LOCK

...OKAY.
WHAT CAN I GET YOU GUYS?

UH...
IT'S SAFE NOW.

UMM, UH...
BANG
BANG BANG
BANG BANG

TWO QUARTERS...
AN AK-47
AND A BLUEBERRY KUSH...

SORRY ABOUT THE BOYS.
THEY'RE IN A WEIRD MOOD.

YEAH, UH... THAT WAS...
... INTENSE.

I GUESS I SHOULD GET 'EM OUT OF THE HOUSE MORE...
THIS STUFF DON'T SELL ITSELF THOUGH...

DID UH, DID YOU GET A DOG, WW?

WHAT? A DOG? NO...

OH, THE SHIT!
NO, NO, THAT'S JUST THE BOYS.

ALRIGHT, HERE YOU GO. $180.
TH-THANKS.

YOU GUYS WANNA HANG AROUND?

I JUST GOT THIS STEVEN SEAGAL BOXSET!

YEAH, UH, WE BETTER BE OFF...
WE GOTTA GET TO THE UH... POST OFFICE... OR SOMETHING...

OH, OKAY... MAYBE NEXT TIME
YEAH, YEAH, FOR SURE...

JESUS FUCKING CHRIST.
THAT WAS HORRIFYING.

I'M GETTING MY TUBES TIED.
I'M GETTING A VASECTOMY.

MEGG, MOGG & OWL

GUYS! COME ON! I WANNA GET IN THERE!

Laser Zone

OPEN

PUFF PUFF PUFF PUFF PUFF PUFF PUFF

WOO! WOO! WOO! WOO!

WE'VE GOTTA GET TO THE BASE AND DEFEND IT!

HANG ON... I NEED TO FINISH MY FRIES.

SECURE THAT CORRIDOR!

UGH, THERE'S KIDS IN HERE.

WHAT?!

FUCK YOU.

FUCK YOU.

ZAP ZAP ZAP ZAP ZAP

FUCK YOU.

GET OUT. THE ADULTS ARE HERE...

OOH! ACE OF BASS! "THE SIGN". I LOVE THIS SONG.

♫ I SAW THE SIGN/ AND IT OPENED UP MY EYES/ I SAW THE SIGN

♫ NO ONE'S GONNA DRAG YOU UP/ TO GET INTO THE LIGHT WHERE YOU BELONG

♫ BUT WHERE DO YOU BE-LO-NG?

!

!

POW

NOOOOOOOOOOO!

!

!

CRASH!

GAME OVER. "BANNED FOR LIFE".

MEGG, BOOGER AND WEREWOLF JONES

OOH, THIS ONE'S NICE.
OH, FUCK YEAH.

CAN WE MOVE THIS ALONG, LADIES?
RACING FORM
I GOTTA GET THIS BET ON.

YEAH, YEAH, YEAH... WE'LL JUST TRY THESE ON.

HELLO, THESE. THANKS.
LADY'S CHANGE ROOM

UH, SORRY... WE UH...
WE DON'T ALLOW MEN IN THE LADY'S CHANGE ROOMS.

WHAT?
HOW FUCKING DARE YOU?!

BOOGER IS NOT A "MAN".
LADY'S CHANGE ROOM
IT'S FINE MEGG, FORGET IT.

LET'S JUST GO.
FUCK YOU, YOU HATE MONGER!

I CAN'T BELIEVE THAT RUDE BITCH!
OH, IT HAPPENS ALL THE TIME...

HOLD UP. I GOTTA PISS. WAIT FOR ME.

CAN'T YOU PISS AT THE BETTING PARLOUR?

YEAH, I DON'T REALLY FEEL LIKE GETTING BEATEN TO DEATH TODAY.
WOO, THAT'S BETTER.
I'VE BEEN HOLDING THAT FOR HOURS.
ARG, WE GOTTA HOOF IT.
I GOT A HOT TIP ON "JINGLE JANGLES" IN THE 5TH...
EWW, GROSS. THAT'S A FUCKING MAN.
EW, GROSS...
YOU'RE A STUPID LITTLE CUNT.
SLAP
C'MON, LADIES...
FUCK THE RACES. LET'S GO GET MANICURES. ON ME.
OOH!
OH, "OUR HERO".

MEGG MOGG AND OWL

UGHN, UGHN, UGHN
POUND POUND POUND
TAP TAP
LET'S STOP FOR A BIT
I'M A BIT BORED.
AND YOU NEED TO TRIM YOUR CLAWS.
SLUG
. . .
MMM. NICE SUNSET.
... YEAH ...
MEGG... UH ... DO YOU EVER WISH I WAS... NOT SO LITTLE?
WE STILL HAVE GOOD SEX DON'T WE?...
WE'RE STILL A TEAM AREN'T WE?
YOU AND ME FOREVER?
OF COURSE...
"FOREVER".

"MEGG, MOGG & OWL"
(+ WEREWOLF JONES)

WOAH... I GOTTA GET OUTTA HERE...

OH, WHERE ARE YOU GOING, OWL?

JUST... OUT.
NOTHING INTERESTING.

UH-HUH.

SO THIS ISN'T YOU?
FEATHERED BANGS
SECRET VALLEY
PRINCE DIRT
YOU'RE NOT PLAYING A "GIG" TONIGHT?

WHY WOULD YOU NOT WANT US TO COME?...
I CAN'T WAIT FOR IT! I BOUGHT THE FIRST TICKET.

"FEATHERED BANGS".
LOL.

...

FUCK.
LOOK, I'M SORRY. BUT THIS IS A BIG DEAL FOR ME.

THERE'S SOME COOL LABEL GUYS AT THIS THING...
AND A GIRL I REALLY WANT TO "IMPRESS"...

MM-HMM.
SNICKER
SEE YOU AT THE SHOW, BUDDY!

...
UM. HI...

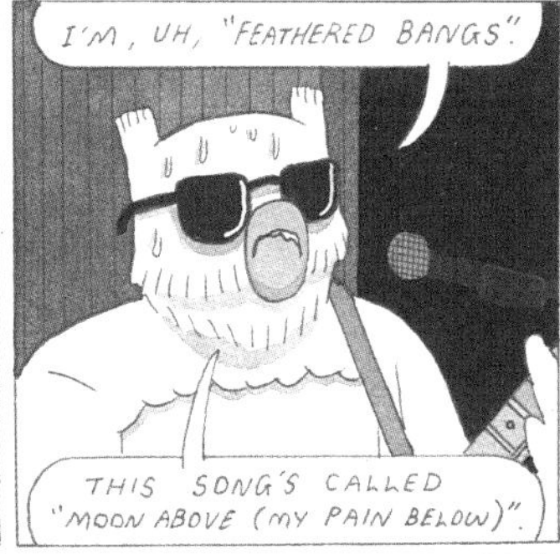
I'M, UH, "FEATHERED BANGS".
THIS SONG'S CALLED "MOON ABOVE (MY PAIN BELOW)".

... ♫ I'VE SEEN SO MANY TOMORROWS TURN INTO YESTERDAYS

♫ LIKE CHILDREN'S LAUGHTER FADES AWAY
FEATHERED BANGS

♫ THESE ARE JUST THE TEARS OF SORROW
RIP

♫ FROM A BAAABY BIIIIRD...
CRUMPLE
UGCH!

♫ THAT'S GONE ASTRAY—
BOOODOOOOOOOOOO.

...♫ GIVE ME JUST ONE MORE CHANCE
WAVE

♫ TO TOUCH THE SKY
SWAY

♫ UNFURL MY WINGS

YOU'RE NOT DRINKING THESE DRINKS ARE YOU?

GO ON... KEEP PLAYING.
♫ A-AND LEARN TO FLY...

OH MY GOD! YOU DICKS!
WHAT THE FUCK?!

WHY COULDN'T YOU JUST LET ME PLAY MY FUCKING SET?!

THAT'S NOT HOW THE SCENE WORKS, OWL.
YEAH, REMEMBER THE TIME I DID MY SOLO PERCUSSION THING AND MEGG STABBED ME?

AND WHEN MEGG DID HER ACAPELLA DANZIG COVERS THING AND I SMASHED A BOTTLE ON HER CROTCH!

THIS IS THE STUFF THAT MAKES OUR SCENE INTERESTING.
OUT OF STATE PEOPLE ARE SCARED TO PLAY HERE.

I FUCKING LOVE THIS SCENE.
FUCK YOUR LADDER-CLIMBING BULLSHIT.

SIGH
WHERE ARE WE GOING?

DOWN TO THE OLD BLEACHERS THAT FACE THE OCEAN!
WITH WINE & CODEINE!

CHEER UP, OWL. YOUR SET WASN'T THAT BAD.
YOUR VOCALS WERE LOW IN THE MIX. THAT WAS GOOD...

NO MORE MUSIC TALK.
LET'S GET FUCKING WASTED.

...LOOK AT THE WATER RIPPLING IN THE BREEZE.
FUCKING BEAUTIFUL...

MEGG
&
MOGG

180 GRAM
SLAYER

BLUUWHRHH!

BRAAAAAAA!

BREOOOOWWW!

ONE HOUR LATER
KICK...
KICK...
KICK...

. . .

OH, HEY...
HEY.
SASSY

WHY ARE YOU ALL SWEATY?
I'VE BEEN WORKING OUT.

. . .
UGH!

MEGG & MOGG
SPIDER MAN
X-MEN

SHINE
SMASH
SMOOTH
GRAPE SODA

HEY.

WHATCHA DOIN'?

DREAMING.

COOL

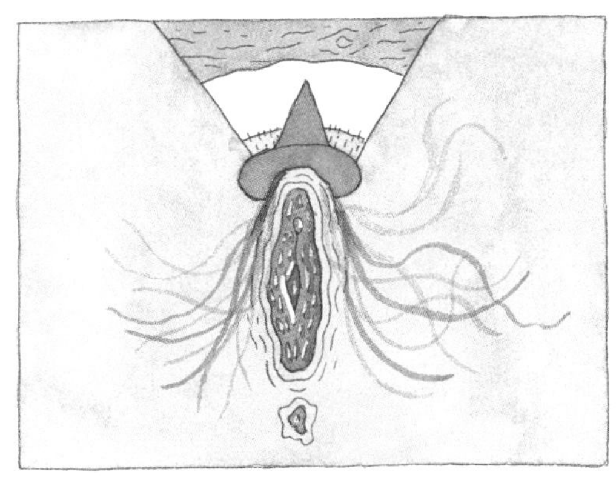

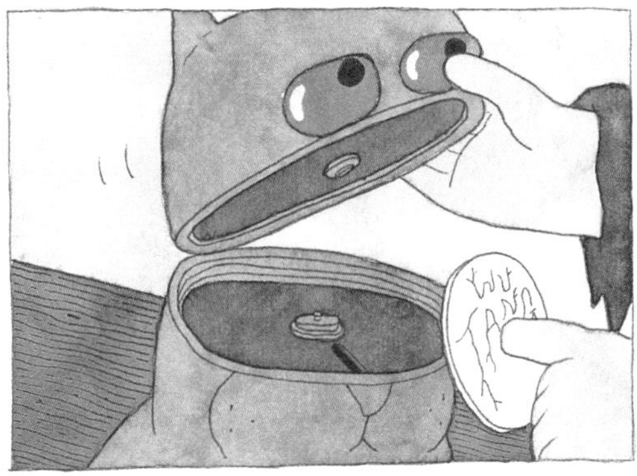
WU

CLICK

TECHNIQUE IS ILL SON
WATCH HOW I SPILL ONE
PEACE TO BIGGIE TUPAC
BIG L & BIG PUN
HAVOC ON
THE STREETS
OF STATIN
SNITCHES
HOUSE NIGGAZ
CHILDREN WATCH
AS THEY PRODUCE
DA SAME PATTERNS

"YOUNG PROFESSIONALS"

MAN, WHAT A CLASSY AFTERNOON!

IT WAS NICE TO GET OUT OF THE HOUSE.

YEAH, GOOD IDEA, MEGG*
* ACTUALLY OWL'S IDEA.

WE SHOULD DO CLASSY PICNICS MORE OFTEN...

SLURP

PUFF

YEAH, I HAD A GOOD TIME.

TOP CLASS!
PRICK

...

"GATORADE™ SAUNA"

GOOD EVENING, MA'AM. THIS IS OWL CALLING FROM THE INDEPENDE-
. . .

!

GOOD LORD!
WHAT?

... I DON'T EVEN WANT TO REPEAT IT...
JUST... FILTH. VILE FILTH.

SIGH
...CLASSLESS TRASH...

OOH! QUITTIN' TIME!

THAT WAS A PRETTY FUCKING AWFUL SHIFT.
TURD SQUAD
UGH, I KNOW... GOD, I HATE PEOPLE SO MUCH.

WHATCHA DOIN' TONIGHT?
OH, NOTHING MUCH, JUST RELAXING... BIT OF TV...

WOAH, I GOTTA RUN! DON'T WANNA MISS THIS TRAIN!
OKAY, HAVE A GOOD NIGHT! SEE YOU TOMORROW!

...I'M IN LOVE WITH YOU...
SIGH

UGH, MOVE YOUR LEGS, YOU RUDE FUCKING JERK!
TURD SQUAD
PONY BOYZ
MAP:
POOTANG CLAN

BAH! COVER YOUR MOUTH WHEN YOU YAWN!
BOORISH SIMPLETON!

UGCH
FUCK MY LIFE.

AHH, HOME SWEET HOME.
TIME TO CATCH UP ON HANNIBAL...

OOH, OR MAYBE THE BACK END OF THE NEW MINDY PROJECT...
OWL'S ROOM

...

WHAT THE F-

!?

OH, HEY, OWL!

WEREWOLF JONES!?!
W-WHAT THE FUCK!?

COME ON IN, DUDE!
WE GOT THIS SHIT CRANKIN'!

I-WHA?! WHAT...
WHAT THE HELL ARE YOU DOING!?!

HOME MADE SAUNA, BRO!

GET ON IN HERE!
JOIN THE PARTY!

DUDE, YOU LOOK STRESSED.
YOU NEED A BACK RUB?

LET DIESEL WORK HIS MAGIC ON YOU...

HE'S GOT HIS MOTHER'S HANDS!

MY CLOTHES! MY PHOTO ALBUMS!
1987-90
EVERYTHING'S ALL STICKY?!

YEAH, WE'RE USING GATORADE!

LET'S DO ANOTHER BLAST!

CHERRY GLACIER OR WATERMELON CHILL?

BOTH!

PSCHHHH!

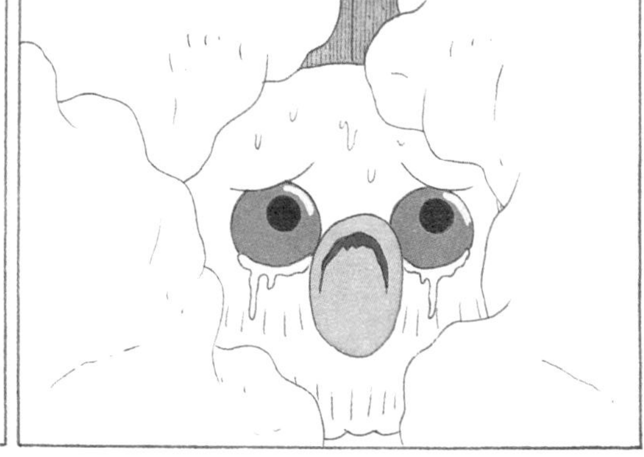

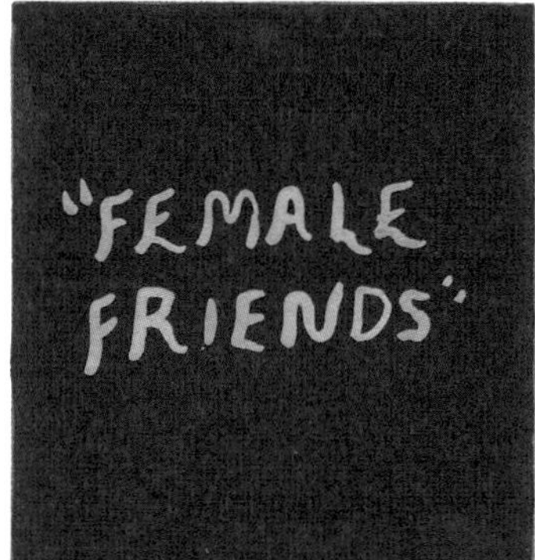
"FEMALE FRIENDS"

FUCK YEAH!
SHOOT HER IN THE FACE!

I'M TRYING! I'M TRYING!
DUMB BITCH WON'T STAY STILL...

SHOOT THAT POLICE HORSE!

BLAM!

WOOOOO!
NICE!

X-BOX
FACE IV
SHOOTER
"RAPETASTIC" -GAMERGATE.

CAN YOU RIP THAT STRIPPER'S CLOTHES OFF?

NO, IT WON'T LET ME.
WELL THAT'S STUPID.

OOH, I CAN STAB HER, THOUGH!
WOAH!

DO YOU WANT A GO, MEGG?

EW, NO.

THIS GAME IS HORRIBLE.

OH, C'MON. IT'S A BIT OF SILLY FUN.
IT'S HARMLESS.

UGH.
THE LAST LEVEL WAS CALLED "FEMINIST RALLY MASSACRE".

...
WHY DON'T I HAVE ANY FEMALE FRIENDS?

YOU'RE OUR ELAINE!

FUCK YOU!
YOU GUYS ARE MY FUCKING ELAINES.

BAH.

HI... BOOGER? IT'S MEGG...
HI.

DO UH... DO YOU WANNA MAYBE DO SOMETHING TODAY?
I DON'T KNOW LIKE~

OH, REALLY ?!
YEAH OKAY!

OKAY, I'LL MEET YOU IN HALF AN HOUR!
LOOKING FORWARD TO IT!

HEY, MEGG!
HEY! HI!

I'M GLAD YOU CALLED!
YEAH?

YEAH, MY SISTER'S PRESSURING ME TO GO TO THIS PARTY THING SHE'S PUTTING ON...

I WARN YOU: I DON'T KNOW WHAT THIS THING'S GONNA BE LIKE...
IT CAN'T BE WORSE THAN WHAT'S GOING ON AT MY HOUSE...

LIQUOR WORLD
HAHAHAHAHA!

OH MY GOD I KNOW RIGHT?
AND THEN HE WAS LIKE "OH, WHOOPS".

FUCKING DUMBASS.
OOOOH! LET'S GET TEQUILLA!

ARE YOU SEEING ANYONE AT THE MOMENT?
BLECH. IT'S COMPLICATED.

I'VE BEEN DOING THE OPEN THING WITH A FEW PEOPLE.

IT'S GOTTEN A BIT MESSY...
I'M NOT REALLY SURE IT'S FOR ME...

MMMM...
HEY, ARE THEY GOING TO HAVE FOOD AT THIS THING?

I'M UH, I'M NOT SURE.
GREASY JOE
I'M PRETTY HUNGRY. DO YOU MIND IF WE STOP HERE?

NO, THAT'S FINE. I COULD DO SOME SLICES.
GREASY JOE
COOL!

...MM-MMM!
CHEEEEEEEESE.

OOOOKAAAY...
HERE IT IS...

BOOGER!
HEY, SIS.

OMG! HOW ARE YOU?!
YEAH, NOT BAD.

THIS IS MY FRIEND, MEGG.
HI, MEGG!

WELCOME TO OUR CRAFTERNOON!

GIRLS, THIS IS MY SISTER, BOOGER!
AND HER FRIEND MEGG!

HI!
HELLO!

THIS IS EMMA, CLARITY AND AZURA!

CLARITY, I THINK YOUR LASAGNA IS DONE!
IT'S SMELLING AWESOME!

CLARITY MADE VEGAN LASAGNA! YUMMO!
OH, UH, WE ALREADY ATE.

OH NO!
YEAH, UH, IT'S FINE.

BASIC WAGES BLAH BLAH BLAH
BLAH BLAH BLAH DETENTION CENTERS.

BLAH BLAH BLAH THE REFUGEES.
DISCRIMINATION BLAH BLAH BLAH.

BLAH BLAH BLAH PRIVILEGE.
BLAH BLAH BLAH YARN BOMBING.

OKAY! LASAGNA'S READY!

HERE YOU GO, MEGG!
WHAT? OH, NO, I ALREADY ATE.

...
OH... OKAY...

OH WOW, THIS IS SO GOOD, CLARITY!
SO TASTY!

SIT ON DOWN, YOU CAN HELP US WITH THESE ACORN ORNAMENTS!

GRAB SOME TOOLS FROM THE PEG BOARD!

...
CAN UH, CAN WE SMOKE IN HERE?

OOH, SORRY, NO. IF YOU COULD SMOKE OUTSIDE THAT WOULD BE GREAT!

JESUS FUCKING CHRIST.

WHAT THE FUCK'S GOING ON?

I'M SORRY, I KIND OF THOUGHT IT MIGHT BE SOMETHING LIKE THIS.

YEAH. THIS UH, THIS REALLY ISN'T MY SCENE.
ME NEITHER.

THEY'RE NICE KIDS BUT UH, YEAH...

ONE HOUR LATER:
FUUUUUUCK

SLAM

I GUESS WE SHOULD GO BACK IN...
I JUST REALLY DON'T THINK I CAN.

SLAM

I JUST REALLY HONESTLY DON'T THINK I CAN

UGH, BUT I REALLY NEED TO PISS.
JUST PISS OUT HERE...

HMMM.
...OKAY...

...

WHAT ARE YOU TWO DOING?

CHAIN SMOKING...

IT'S NICE OUT HERE.

YOU SHOULD COME INSIDE!
COME AND PLAY WITH US!

"PLAY"?
WHAT ARE YOU FUCKING FIVE YEARS OLD?

STEADY, MEGG...

I-I THINK YOU REALLY HURT CLARITY'S FEELINGS BEFORE...

WHY DIDN'T YOU EAT ANY OF HER LASAGNA?
SHE WORKED REALLY HARD ON IT...

WHAT THE HELL ARE YOU TALKING ABOUT?!

I ATE A WHOLE PIZZA BEFORE I CAME HERE!
I WASN'T HUNGRY!

I DON'T KNOW... IT'S JUST KIND OF MAKING ME SAD...

WHAT?!
WHAT FUCKING BUSINESS IS IT OF YOURS?!

WHY THE FUCK DO YOU CARE?
I DON'T HAVE TO EAT HER FUCKING VEGAN BULLSHIT!

IT'S JUST... SHE WORKED SO HARD...

OOOOOKAY.
THAT'S JUST FUCKING RIDICULOUS.

GET THE FUCK OUT OF HERE.
JUST... WALK AWAY.

I - I -

JUST WALK THE FUCK AWAY.

THAT'S IT.
KEEP GOING...

UH-HUH. UP THE STEPS.
ALMOST THERE...

GOOD GOD.
HAHA!

OH MY GOD, THAT WAS BRILLIANT!

SHIT.
I'M GOING TO BE IN SO MUCH TROUBLE.

WITH THOSE FLACCID HIPPIES?
WHAT ARE THEY GOING TO DO? WHINE AT YOU TO "PLAY" WITH THEM?

OH NO!

OKAY, LET'S GET THE FUCK OUT OF HERE.
HAHA, OKAY.

WE NEED MORE BOOZES...
SMASH

GET HER!

SHOOT HER IN THE TITS!
YEEEEAAHHH!

ANOTHER "COCKSUCKING COWBOY" BOOGER?
OOH, YES PLEASE!

SPLASH!

WHOOPS!
HAHAHA!

"CAM-BOY DIESEL"

YOU GUYS ORDER ANYTHING YOU WANT!

IT'S ALL ON DIESEL!
SLAYER

WHAT?
REALLY?

YEAH, HIS CAMMING IS BLOWING UP!
WE'RE MAKING A TON OF MONEY!

WHY CAN'T YOU BE MORE LIKE YOUR BROTHER, JAXON?
...

WHA!?!
"CAMMING"?!

FOR GOD'S SAKE, WEREWOLF JONES!
HE'S TEN YEAR'S OLD!!

THAT'S NOT WHAT HIS PROFILE SAYS...

WINK

NO, BUT SERIOUSLY, IT'S FINE.
IT'S ALL ABOVE BOARD.

THIS IS PORN BY KIDS FOR KIDS.
IT'S HUGE IN JAPAN.

HE STARTED OFF A T-BACK JUNIOR IDOL.
THEN WE MOVED HIM ONTO THE CAM'.

IT'S... "LEGAL".

AND WE ARE MAKING A LOT OF CA$H!
AREN'T WE, BUDDY?!

... DRINKS ON ME!

FIVE MOJITOS, PLEASE.
I'LL HAVE A TRIPLE JAMESON, NO ICE.
...

MEGG, MOGG, OWL AND WEREWOLF JONES.

UGH, JUST LET US ON, YOU PRICK. IT'S FUCKING FREEZING.
BUS

OH MY GOD... DID YOU SEE THAT GUY WITH THE FACE SCAR?
I'M REALLY ACTUALLY SCARED.

CALM THE FUCK DOWN, OWL.
NOBODY'S GETTING DECAPITATED.

... I HAD A DREAM THAT ONE OF US DIES ON THIS TRIP.
...

NO WAY! THIS IS GONNA BE THE BEST!
1000 BANDS ACROSS 2000 STAGES IN THE MIDDLE OF NOWHERE!

WOOOOOOOO!!

WHO ARE YOU MOST EXCITED TO SEE, WEREWOLF JONES?

...

NAH, MAN.
I KEEP MY MUSIC TASTES CLOSE TO MY CHEST.

THAT SHIT'S PERSONAL...

AND I DON'T WANT TO HEAR ABOUT ALL THE NERDY SHIT YOU WANNA SEE.
DON'T MAKE ME LOSE EVEN MORE RESPECT FOR YOU, OWL.

BANG!
WOAH!

WHAT THE FUCK WAS THAT?!

SORRY, FOLKS... WE-WE JUST HIT A DEER...

YEP... HE'S DEAD...
BOLT BUS

WE BETTER DRAG HIM OFF THE ROAD.

OH, THAT'S HORRIBLE. HE'S SO BEAUTIFUL...

PUT HIM IN THE CARGO. I'LL PAY THE CHARGES.

I CAN COOK HIM UP... HE WON'T GO TO WASTE.

OOH, THAT SOUNDS NICE!
LET'S DO THAT!

ANIMALS ARE GOOD FOR TWO THINGS. EATIN' AND FUCKIN'.
AMEN TO THAT!

OKAY, WE'LL BE BACK ON THE ROAD NOW... SORRY ABOUT THAT, FOLKS...

BANG
BANG
BANG

WHAT THE HECK IS THAT?!

RIP

CRASH

FUCK...

THAT WAS BRUTAL.

I'M SORRY, FOLKS, IT LOOKS LIKE WE'RE GOING TO BE HERE A WHILE.

UGCH! THE FIRST BAND STARTS IN AN HOUR.

... YOU GUYS ARE GOING TO THE FESTIVAL?
YEAH!

I GOT MY BUDDY ON THE WAY.
...WE CAN GIVE YOU A RIDE...

THAT'D BE FUCKIN' GREAT. FUCK YEAH.

...

GUYS. I'M REALLY FREAKING OUT... I DON'T LIKE THIS.

I SWEAR THIS GUY IS GOING TO KILL US...
THERE'S SOMETHING WRONG WITH HIM...

SHUT UP, OWL. BLADE IS A TOTAL SWEET-HEART.
DON'T BE A CUNT.

OOH! I HEAR MUSIC!
WE'RE GETTING CLOSE!

THERE. YOU SEE, OWL.

EVERYTHING'S FINE.

...
THIS ISN'T THE PITCHFORK FESTIVAL...

GUYS, THIS IS THE FUCKING GATHERING!
THIS IS WORSE THAN BURNING MAN!
OOH, THEY HAVE A "DRUG BRIDGE"!
DRUG BRIDGE
OH!
OOOH! CLOWN BURLESQUE!
YOU FOLKS HUNGRY?
WE'RE COOKIN' UP.
WOW... THIS IS DELICIOUS, BLADE.
THE HOSPITALITY OF THE PSYCHOPATHIC FAMILY IS TRULY UNPARALLELED.
THERE'S WASPS EVERYWHERE!
OH GOD...
I'M SITTING IN A FECES!
OKAY... ARE WE GONNA FUCK NOW?
OR DO I GOTTA GET NASTY?
24 HR MOTEL
ROOM FOR FOUR, PLEASE...
THIS SUCKS...
I KNOW. I'M MISSING BILLY CORGAN.
UGCH.
YOU'RE SLEEPING ON THE FLOOR.
SHOVE
I'M SERIOUS.

MEGG, MOGG & OWL

MNGH...

UGH.
GOOD MORNING.

WHAT TIME IS IT?

FUCK.
2 AM.

BLECH. WE NEED TO FIX OUR SLEEPING PATTERN.

WHAT ARE YOU GETTING?
HOT DOG. YOU?

SEXY DONUTS.

HEY, STEVEN. HOW YOU DOIN'?
YEAH, NOT TOO BAD. SAME OLD, SAME OLD.

SIGH
WE HAVE GOT TO STOP EXCLUSIVELY EATING AT THE 7...

AH, FUCK!

WHAT?
UGH.

IT'S THE FUCKING HOT DOG WITH THE OPEN PACKAGING.
I'VE BEEN AVOIDING THIS ONE FOR DAYS.

FUCK... I DON'T WANT TO GO BACK.
I'M SURE IT'LL BE OKAY...

THE EXPIRATION DATE'S STILL GOOD...

FUMBLE

OH, GODDAMMIT. MY WEINER.
HAHAHAHAHAHA.

IT WAS ALREADY HALF OPEN.
NICE WORK.

I'LL JUST RINSE IT IN THE SINK.

THE MICROWAVE'LL BURN OFF ANY EXTRA GERMS...
HUUUMMMM

SNIFF

IT SMELLS OKAY...

HMMM.
THE UH, THE BUN'S A BIT ROPEY.

EH, IT SEEMS FINE...
"HOORAY"

ONE HOUR LATER:
OHHHHH FUUUUUUUCK.

SOB

JESUS...
WHAT THE FUCK'S GOING ON IN HERE?

IT'S 3AM.

MEGG BOUGHT THE OPEN HOT DOG AND THEN IT FELL ON THE FLOOR.
HUMP

MOOOOOAN

...

YOU GUYS REALLY NEED TO GET YOUR SHIT TOGETHER...
THIS - THIS IS REALLY PATHETIC.

MEGG AND MOGG
HEY, DUDES. I'M OFF TO THE GYM.
UGH. MAKE SURE YOU SHOWER BEFORE YOU COME HOME THIS TIME.
WHAT?...
UH, OKAY...
WOO. PLACE TO OURSELVES.
YOU, UH, YOU WANNA FOOL AROUND?...
DO YOU WANT ME TO GO DOWN ON YOU FOR A BIT?
UH... YEAH...
BUT DO YOU UH–
DO YOU THINK UH, MAYBE YOU MIGHT... EAT MY BUTT?
... RIM YOU?
REALLY?
YEAH, UH, I DON'T KNOW.
THAT'S NOT REALLY SOMETHING I WANT TO DO...
...
THERE'S A LOT OF HAIR DOWN THERE...
YEAH, I - I DON'T THINK I CAN...
SORRY.
NOT EVEN FOR JUST LIKE A MINUTE?
I JUST NEED TO KNOW WHAT IT FEELS LIKE.
I'M SORRY, I REALLY CAN'T.
UGH.

YOU'RE SO VANILLA...
WHAT?!
I AM NOT!
HA. OH YEAH...
YOU'RE TOTALLY WILD.
THERE.
I SHAVED MY BUTT.
C'MON! JUST FOR ONE MINUTE.
I GAVE IT A DEEP CLEANSE.
IT'S IMMACULATE.
FOR FUCK'S SAKE.
FINE.
SERIOUSLY. ONE MINUTE.
I JUST HAVE TO KNOW...
LOOK, SEE. IT'S SOOOO CLEAN.
AND I RUBBED A LITTLE BROWN SUGAR ON THERE.
IT'S A SWEET TASTY TREAT!

UH HUH.
...
YOU HAVE A NOODLE ON YOUR ASS.
PICK
A NOODLE?

ARGH!!
WHAT?
IT'S A FUCKING WORM!

THERE'S NO WAY IT WAS A WORM.
NO FUCKING WAY.
I KNOW A WORM WHEN I SEE ONE!

USE THIS CANDY WRAPPER AS A DAM...
C'MON, THIRTY SECONDS. PLEASE!
≡ SIGH ≡

MEGG & MOGG
THAT WAS OKAY...
MEH.
THEY WERE PRETTY FUCKING BORING.
WE MAY AS WELL HAVE JUST LISTENED TO THE ALBUM AT HOME.
UGH.
20 MINUTES. GROSS.
FUCK...
I NEED TO SHIT.
I GOT GURGLING BEER-GUTS...
I'M TOTALLY GOING TO SHIT MYSELF...
I DON'T THINK THERE'S A TOILET DOWN HERE.
FUCK.
ALRIGHT... KEEP AN EYE OUT FOR PIGS...
SLIDE
WHA?
YOU'RE POOPING HERE?
YEAH, KEEP YOUR VOICE DOWN.
ACT CASUAL...

WIPE

WIPE

...

MAN! ...
THAT WAS FUCKING INCREDIBLE!

OH MY GOD I'M SO IN LOVE WITH YOU!

TWO WIPES!
YOU'RE SO CLASSY!

ALRIGHT, WHATEVER...

NO, I AM BLOWN AWAY.
THAT WAS SLICK.

I SERIOUSLY COULD NOT BE MORE IN LOVE WITH YOU RIGHT NOW.

... WOW.

MEGG
AND
MOGG
SMACK

OHHHHHHHHHH...

SMACK
OHHHHH!

SNIFF
FUCK... WE NEED TO SHUT THIS DOWN.

WE SHOULD GET BACK TO THE PARTY...

IT'S JUST A BIT OF LIGHT SPANKING...
THIS ISN'T CHEATING.

NO, I NEED TO LEAVE...
OTHERWISE I'LL FUCK YOU.

ARE YOU SURE? I LITERALLY JUST WASHED MY DICK.
...IT WAS A CHAMOMILE AND YLANG-YLANG BODYSCRUB...

UGCH.
GROSS.

♥MEGG!♥
WHERE WERE YOU? YOU MISSED THE END OF EPISODE 18! WE'RE ONTO DISC 5! HOUR 16! HAVE MORE COFFEE!

WHA? ... OKAY, COOL. WHATEVER...

ARE YOU OKAY?
YOU SEEM "BLAH".

YEAH, I'M FINE. I'M JUST GETTING TIRED.

WELL, ONLY ABOUT 12 HOURS TO GO...

WOOOOOOOOOO!!

GOD, EVERYBODY JUST GET THE FUCK OUT OF MY HOUSE.

...
MMMMM

HEY, MEGG, DO YOU WANT TO-

WHAT HAPPENED TO YOUR BUTT?
...

I UH, I SAT DOWN TOO FAST...
ON ONE OF THE KITCHEN CHAIRS.

...

MEGG,
MOGG
& OWL

GODDAMMIT!

TOWELS ALL OVER THE FLOOR!

SHIT STAINS ALL OVER THE TOILET BOWL!

JUNK ALL OVER THE FLOOR!

UGH. THIS BUCKET BONG STINKS!

GOOD LORD! A DILDO?!
ON THE FUCKING KITCHEN TABLE!

ARGH! CRUMBS IN MY GOOD BUTTER!
HOW MANY TIMES HAVE I —

FILTH! FILTH EVERYWHERE!

I CAN'T LIVE LIKE THIS ANYMORE...

QUIT WHINING, OWL.

NOTHING MATTERS. EVERYTHING IS MEANINGLESS.
STOP TRYING SO HARD.

MEGG... WHERE HAVE YOU BEEN?
HEY, "DOWN IN FRONT".

SHOVE OVER.

...
WHERE WERE YOU?

NOWHERE... I WAS JUST- I WAS...
I WAS HAVING MY "WINTER ABORTION"...

OH... FUCK...
... SORRY.

IT'S NOBODY'S FAULT...
IT GETS COLD IN WINTER...

NOW IT'S SPRING BRISKET TIME!
OOH, BRISKET!

MMMMMM!!

?
?
?

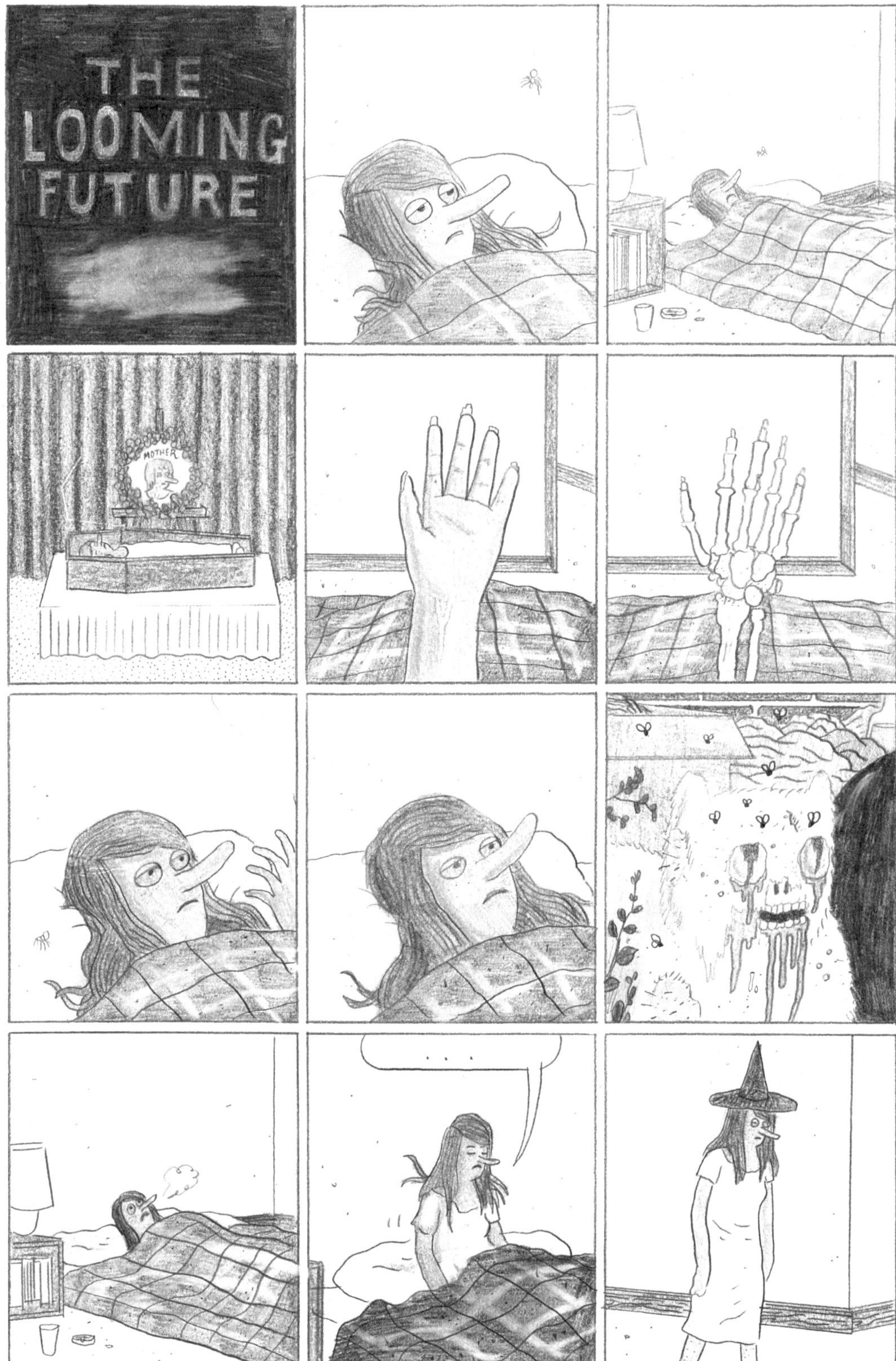
THE LOOMING FUTURE
MOTHER
. . .

FLIP
CLICK
HEY, MEGG.
DO YOU WANT TO COME TO THE PARK?
...I'VE GOT A HIP-FLASK FULL OF METHODONE...
YEAH... OKAY.
SNAP

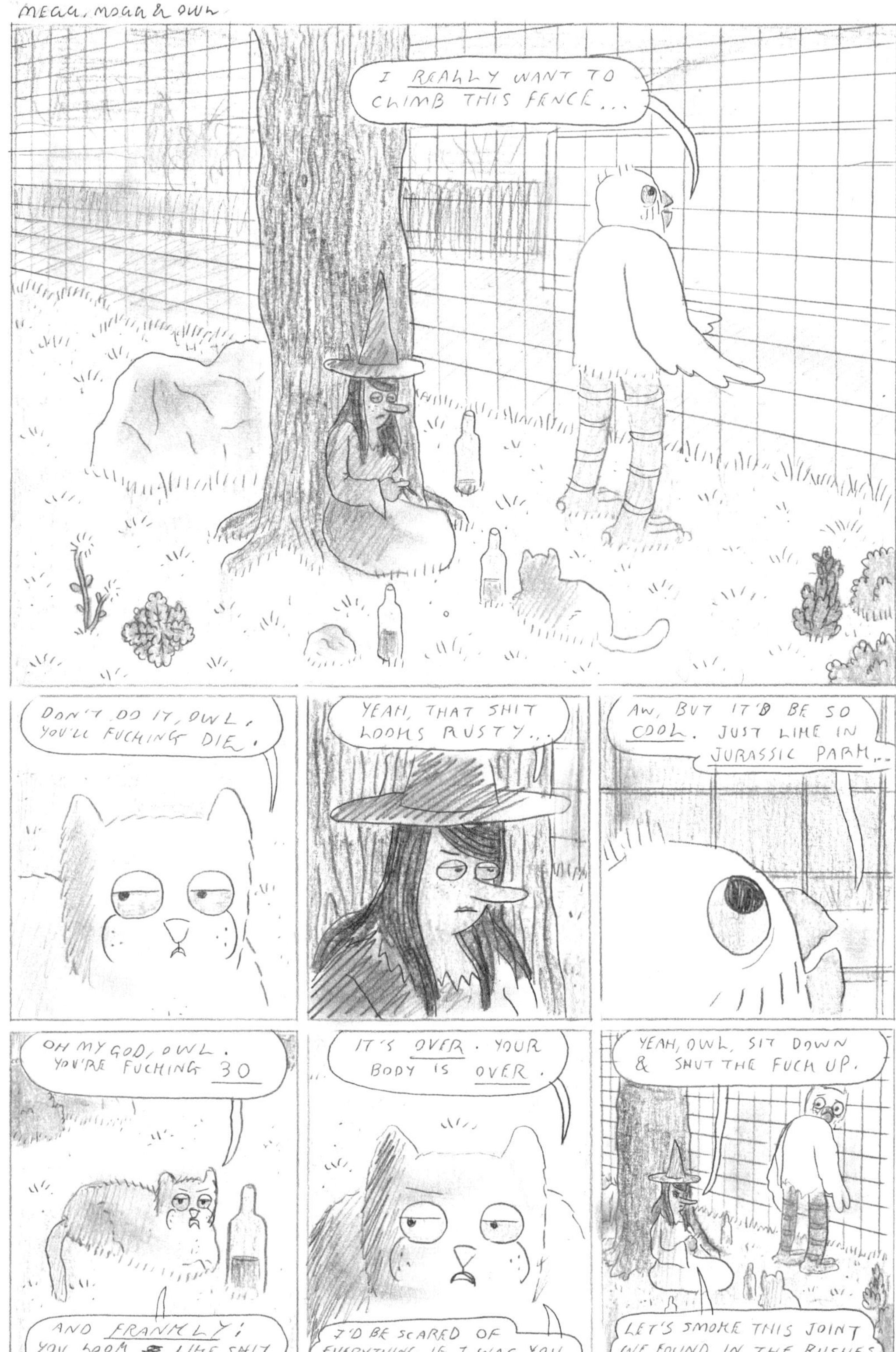
I REALLY WANT TO CLIMB THIS FENCE...
DON'T DO IT, OWL. YOU'LL FUCKING DIE.
YEAH, THAT SHIT LOOKS RUSTY...
AW, BUT IT'D BE SO COOL. JUST LIKE IN JURASSIC PARK...
OH MY GOD, OWL. YOU'RE FUCKING 30
AND FRANKLY, YOU LOOK LIKE SHIT.
IT'S OVER. YOUR BODY IS OVER.
I'D BE SCARED OF EVERYTHING IF I WAS YOU.
YEAH, OWL, SIT DOWN & SHUT THE FUCK UP.
LET'S SMOKE THIS JOINT WE FOUND IN THE BUSHES.

"QATAR
FELT HAT
EXPO"

YOU BOYS ALMOST DONE WITH THAT LAST BATCH?!

I'M TIRED, DADDY.

MY HANDS HURT.

UGH, C'MON YOU CAN DO IT.
THIS IS VERY IMPORTANT FOR DADDY.

HERE. HAVE SOME MORE FROOT LOOPS.

FROOT LOOPS
MONSTER

YAY!
HANG ON, HANG ON.

DON'T FORGET YOUR SUGAR.
BUDGET SUGAR

YOU BOYS EAT UP QUICK AND GET BACK TO WORK OKAY.
THIS SHOW IS MAKE OR BREAK.

THIS IS THE BIG ONE.
DADDY'S BEEN TRYING TO BOOK THIS ONE FOR YEARS NOW.

DON'T FUCK THIS UP FOR ME...

SKY BUS

TERMIN

OKAY, RUNNING RIGHT ON SCHEDULE...
LET'S GO DROP OFF THESE HATS.

ANY EXPLOSIVES OR SHARP OBJECTS?
NO, NO. JUST HATS.

DADDY! DADDY! CAN WE HAVE McDONALD'S?!
McDONALDS
OH, DADDY, PLEEEEASE?!

NO, NO, BOYS. DADDY'S NOT MADE OF MONEY.
MEN

NOW, C'MON. INTO THE BAGS.

TAKE YOUR PILLS FIRST...

DO WE REALLY HAVE TO GO IN THE BAGS, DADDY?

YES. YOU'RE THE ONES WHO WERE WHINING FOR NEW SHOES LAST MONTH.

I TOLD YOU THEN AND I'LL TELL YOU NOW: IF YOU WANT SHOES WITHOUT HOLES, YOU HAVE TO GO IN THE BAGS.
NOW TAKE YOUR FUCKING PILLS.

THERE WE GO...
STROKE
MASSAGE
GOOD BOYS.

OH, MAN. THIS IS IT!
I'M SO FUCKING PUMPED!

TIME FOR MY TRAMADOLS...

DADDY, I HAVE TO GO TO THE TOILET.

SHUT UP, JAXON.
WE'RE ABOUT TO GO THROUGH SECURITY.

YOU'LL JUST HAVE TO HOLD IT.
GO TO FUCKING SLEEP.

REMOVE ALL JEWELRY, BELTS OFF, LAPTOPS IN A SEPERATE TRAY...

WHAT'S IN THESE TRASH BAGS, SIR?
UH... TRASH...

MOOOOAAANN

...
WHAT THE?

GODDAMMIT, JAXON, YOU COULDN'T KEEP YOUR FUCKING TRAP SHUT FOR FIVE MINUTES?
GROOOANN

WHAT'S GOING ON HERE?
THIS GUY'S GOT HIS KIDS IN THESE BAGS.

SIR, CHILDREN OVER TWO MUST HAVE SEATS OF THEIR OWN.
GAH!

WELL I CAN'T AFFORD EXTRA FUCKING SEATS!
FOR FUCK'S SAKE!

WAIT, WAIT... THAT ONE'S TWO YEARS OLD...
THE OTHER ONE'S ONE AND A HALF.

SIR, THESE CHILDREN ARE CLEARLY IN THEIR TWEENS...

NAH, NAH, NAH, THEY'RE JUST BIG MEATY MOTHER FUCKERS...
THEY'RE BABIES, I JUST FEED THEM LOTS OF DRUGS!

WHAT'S LEAKING OUT OF YOUR BAG THERE, SIR?
WHAT? OH, FUCK.

IT'S JUST LUBE.
...

SLIM JIMS?

YEAH, WHAT'S THE BIG DEAL?! I TRAVEL WITH A LOT OF SLIM JIMS AND LUBE.
I KNOW MY RIGHTS AS A CITIZEN!

IT'S NOT LIKE I'VE GOT A FUCKING BOMB ON ME!!

OKAY, YOU'LL HAVE TO COME WITH ME, SIR.

WHAT?! NO, I HAVE TO MAKE THIS FLIGHT!
YOU GOTTA FIDDLE AROUND IN MY ASS?...

JUST FUCKEN DO IT HERE.
RIP!
RIP!

GO ON, CHECK ME OUT.

YOU DON'T NEED A GLOVE. I'M CLEAN.

CLEANEST POOPER IN THE BUSINESS.

WHAT THE FUCK ARE YOU LOOKING AT?

OKAY, C'MON, LET'S GO.
HEY! GET YOUR HANDS OFF OF ME!

FUCKING AIR-PIGS!
THIS IS JEANETTE, CAN I GET EXTRA SECURITY OVER HERE?

FOR GOD'S SAKE! JUST LOOK IN MY ASS!
GODDAMMIT!!!

OH, WOAH... THESE TRAMMYS ARE KICKING IN...

MNGHHH

FLAUWMGGHMHN
MNGHW... BUH.

FWOOF.

PPTPDH FFFFFF.
MAAAHNMAAAH...

...

ZZZZZZZZ

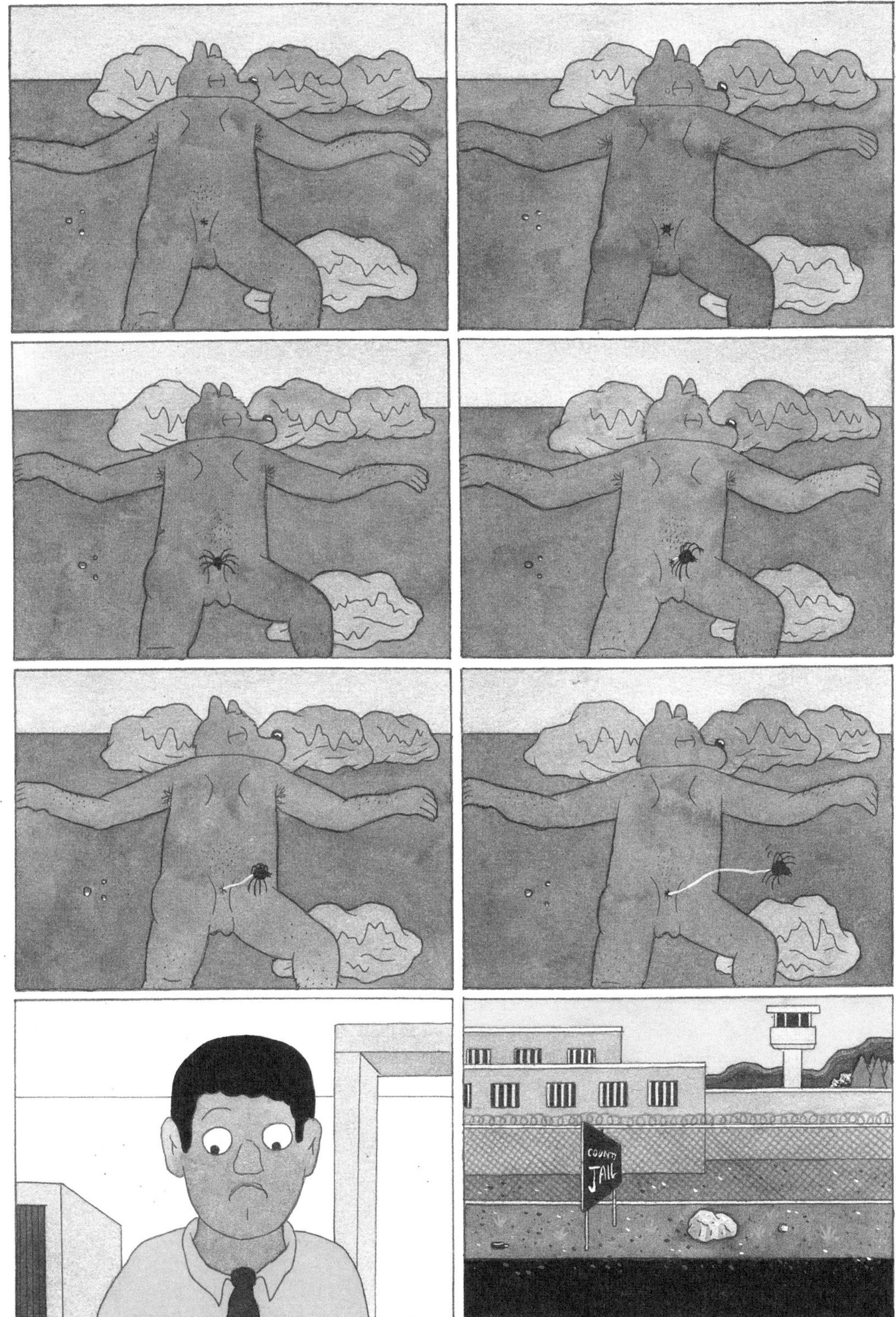
COUNTY
JAIL

HELLO, DADDY...
78341
BOYS!

ARE YOU OKAY, DADDY?

YEAH, YEAH, YEAH, I'M FINE. WHATEVER.

HOW'S THE ETSY!?!

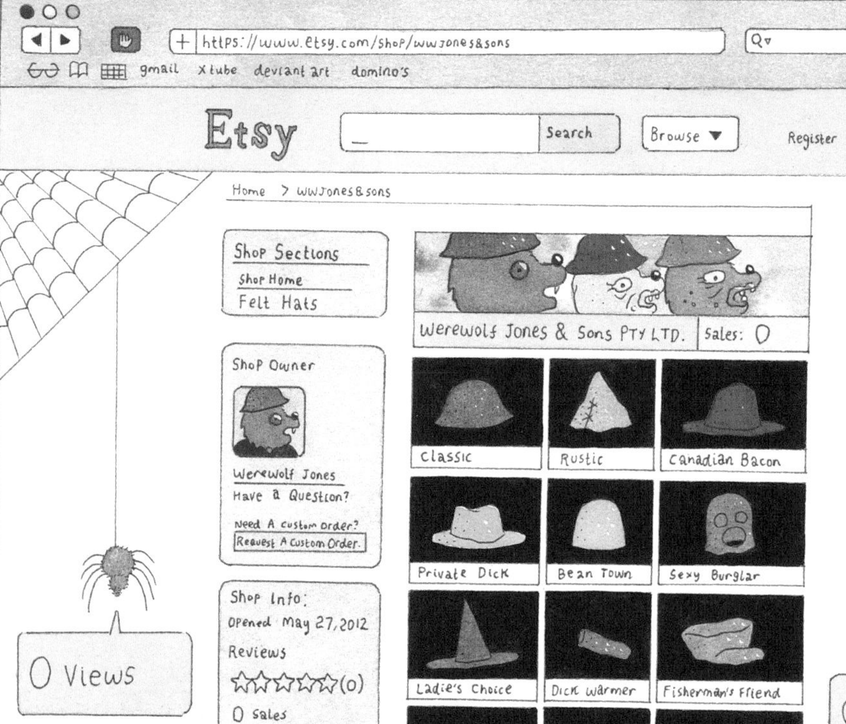
https://www.etsy.com/shop/wwjones&sons
gmail
xtube
deviant art
domino's
Etsy
Search
Browse
Register
Sign In
Cart
Home > wwjones&sons
Shop Sections
Shop Home
Felt Hats
Werewolf Jones & Sons PTY LTD.
Sales: 0
Classic
Rustic
Canadian Bacon
Shop Owner
Werewolf Jones
Have a Question?
Need A custom order?
Request A Custom Order.
Private Dick
Bean Town
Sexy Burglar
Shop Info:
Opened May 27, 2012
Reviews
(0)
0 Sales
0 Admirers
Ladie's Choice
Dick Warmer
Fisherman's Friend
0 Views
0 Sales

"SEX TOWELS"

WHA? WHAT THE FUCK?

WHERE ARE ALL MY TOWELS?

KNOCK KNOCK
KNOCK

MEGG! MOGG!
WHERE ARE ALL MY FUCKING TOWELS?!

I NEED TO SHOWER!
I'VE GOT A TINDER DATE!

WHA?
WHAT'S GOING ON?

WHERE ARE ALL MY FUCKING TOWELS?

JEEZ, I DUNNO...

WE MIGHT HAVE A COUPLE OF THEM?

JESUS CHRIST, MEGG!
UGH!

CAN YOU PUT THAT THING AWAY?
COVER IT UP!

OH FOR FUCK'S SAKE, OWL IT'S JUST A DICK...

WE'VE ALL GOT ONE.

...

W-WHERE ARE MY TOWELS?

ALRIGHT, ALRIGHT, I'LL GET 'EM.
WAIT OUT HERE...

CLICK
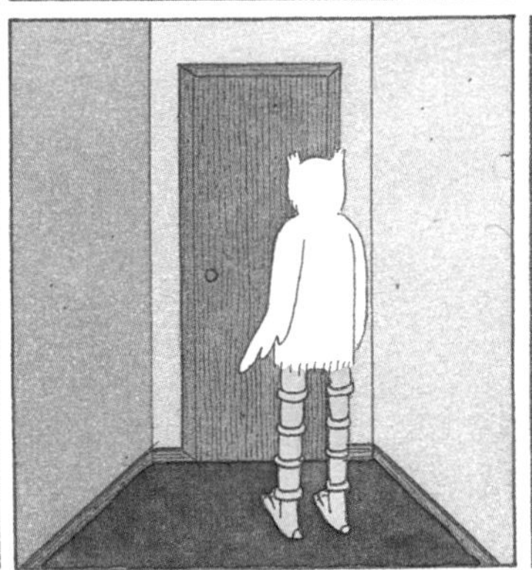

GODDAMMIT.
I'M IN A RUSH!

WHA- WHAT THE FUCK?!

THERE THEY ARE, OWL.
HEY, OWL... SORRY...

MEGG, MOGG & OWL

ARGH!

UGCH.

MOOOAN

SOB

ARE YOU OKAY, MEGG?

YEAH... JUST MY DAILY "BODY FREAKOUT".
I FUCKING HATE BEING IN THIS THING.

MMM...
I'M ACTUALLY FEELING PRETTY GOOD TODAY.

WELL, HOW WONDERFUL FOR YOU.

... I'M A DISGUSTING PERSON...

I'M HAVING A "DISGUSTING PERSON FREAKOUT".
GOD, I FUCKING LOATHE MYSELF.

... I UH, I FEEL FAIRLY NEUTRAL TODAY...
I'M SLIGHTLY TREPIDACIOUS ABOUT THIS SEMINAR I'M ATTEN-

OH FOR FUCK'S SAKE, OWL!
SHUT UP ABOUT YOUR HORRIBLE BORING SEMINARS.

... EVERYBODY JUST SHUT THE FUCK UP.

DRAMA

OH, MAN! CANDY, CANDY, CANDY!

UH-HUH, YEP... GOIN' TO THE CANDY STORE...
WOO!

...
WHA? THIS ISN'T THE CANDY DISTRICT...

HELLO, MEGG!
AND THIS MUST BE MOGG.

COME IN, COME IN...
WHAT THE FUCK'S GOING ON?

COUPLES THERAPY?!
WHAT?

OOOOOKAY.
WINE?

UH, NO, THANK YOU.
I'LL HAVE A FUCKING WINE.

SO, MOGG... MEGG'S TOLD ME A LOT ABOUT YOU...

MM-HMM.

MAYBE WE SHOULD START WITH YOUR BOUNDARY ISSUES?

MY WHAT?

ARE YOU ALMOST DONE, MARIE?

WE'RE JUST GETTING STARTED, TONY.
BUT COME IN.

COOL.

HI.
WHA? WHO THE FUCK IS THIS GUY?

THIS IS TONY, HE'S A SPIRITUAL MASSAGE THERAPIST.
I'D BE INTERESTED IN HIS OPINION.

I SLEEP ON THIS COUCH.

...

CAN I OFFER YOU A MASSAGE?

HEY, UH, MARIE... HAVE YOU SEEN THE-
OH, HELLO!

WHOOPS.
I SHOULD'VE PUT SOME PANTS ON. HAHA.

IT'S OKAY, BILL.
IN FACT MAYBE YOU COULD WEIGH IN ON THIS?

OF COURSE, OF COURSE.
IS THIS THE RIMMING CAT?

OOOOKAY, THAT'S IT. I'M OUT OF HERE.

THIS IS FUCKING CREEPY.
THIS HOUSE STINKS OF SEMEN AND BEARDS.

ARE YOU COMING, MEGG?

...

THIS IS WEIRD.
THIS IS A VERY WEIRD AMBUSH. I'M VERY HIGH.

ME TOO.
I FEEL LIKE I'M GOING TO VOMIT...

WELL I'M LEAVING.
I HAVE TO GO.

I'VE BEEN SLEEPING WITH BOOGER!
!

I THINK I'M MAYBE IN LOVE WITH HER...
I'M CONFUSED...

I - I DON'T WANT YOU AND I TO-
I ~

AMSTERDAM

...

HELLO?

GUYS?...

...WHAT ARE YOU DOING?

PACKING.
WE'RE GOING TO FUCKING AMSTERDAM!

WOOOOOOOOO!

AMSTERDAM?! WHAT?
HOW CAN YOU AFFORD THAT?

WE BOOKED THE TICKETS AAAAAGES AGO...
1998.

OH...
I WANT TO GO TO AMSTERDAM...

SORRY, IT'S A COUPLES THING.

YEAH, IT'S FOR COUPLES.

OH, WELL...
I GUESS I'LL HAVE THE PLACE TO MYSELF FOR A BIT...

SOME "QUALITY ME TIME"...
...

MAN, OWL'S BEEN SO FUCKING CLINGY RECENTLY.

I KNOW...
I'M GLAD TO SEE THE BACK OF HIM.

YEAH. COUPLES TIME.
THIS'LL BE GOOD.

OKING ROOM
SMOKING ROOM

≡SIGH≡ I WISH YOU COULD STILL SMOKE ON PLANES...
IT'S A NATIONAL DISGRACE.

... YOU GOT YOUR BOARDING PASS?
YEAH.
LET'S DO IT.

HAPPY HOUR ALL DAY
COCKTAIL TIME
24 HRS
OKAY...

WE'VE GOT THE VALIUMS FOR NOW.

AND A MOGADON AND PAXODORM FOR THE LAYOVER.
COOL.

"DOWN THE HATCH."

MMM... THIS IS A GOOD COCKTAIL.
YEAH. IT'S STRONG

12 HOURS LATER:
MNGHNHGH

WHA?... WHERE?...
...

TAP TAP TAP
HUH? WHA?

OOH! 20 MINUTES 'TIL LANDING.
NICE!... WHOA. WHO VOMITED EVERYWHERE?

GAH, THAT STEWARD DIDN'T HAVE TO BE SO RUDE.

I DIDN'T KNOW I'D VOMITED.
IT WASN'T MY FAULT.

OOOOH! HERE'S ONE!

THANK GOD.
I'M FEELING HORRIBLY LUCID.

HMMM...
UH, HI...

CAN WE GET SOME "WHITE WEDDING", SOME "NORTHERN WIDOW", SOME "GOVENOR'S RESERVE"...
AND SOME... "SCROOGE McWEED".

MMMM
I'M SO FUCKING HAPPY.

PUFF
PUFF
PUFF

MMMMMM

HEH.
SHIIIIIIT.

OKAY: LET'S GET TO THE HOTEL AND CHECK IN.
ARGH, FUCK. IT'S REALLY COLD.

BRRRRRRR, IT IS...
LET'S GET THE COATS OUT...

WHA? ... WHERE ARE THE COATS?
THIS IS JUST A BUNCH OF PILLOWCASES...

THERE'S SOME SCARY JOCKS ACROSS THE CANAL STARING AT US...
LIKE THEY WANT TO EAT US ALIVE...

HEY, WHAT THE FUCK?
DID YOU FORGET TO PACK YOUR ANTI-DEPRESSANTS? AND MINE?

* MASTURBATING

...OH, FUCK FUCK FUCK FUCK

CAN WE TURN THIS OFF?! I DON'T KNOW WHERE I AM...

WHAT YEAR IS IT?
That '70s Show
WHAT'S GOING ON?

OH MY GOD! THIS ROOM IS "AFFECTIONATELY" KNOWN AS THE... "MURDER ROOM".
HOTEL INFO

"13 SCHOOLGIRLS WERE BRUTALLY SLAIN ON THIS BED IN 1872"
"AND THEY TURN UP AT NIGHT AND BRAID YOUR HAIR"

WHAT?!
OH, FUCK THAT!

...
FUFF
(WHAT WAS THAT?)

...

(I THINK THERE'S SOMETHING IN THE CLOSET.)
(WHAT?! ... WE NEED TO GET THE FUCK OUT OF HERE!)

(I CAN'T GO OUTSIDE!)
(I DON'T WANT TO GO OUTSIDE.)

(WE HAVE TO!)
(THIS ROOM IS FUCKED!)
(AND WE NEED TO FIND A DOCTOR!)

(NO WE DON'T, I'M FINE WITHOUT MY ANTIDEPRESSANTS.)
(I'M FINE. WE'RE FINE.)

(IT'S ALL FUCKING FINE.)

...
...

OKAY...

YOU WERE RIGHT...
THAT ROOM WAS FUCKED.

I NEED MY ANTIDEPRESSANTS.
WHAT THE FUCK ARE WE GOING TO DO?

I DON'T KNOW? WHERE ARE WE?

OVERLIJDEN STREET...
WHAT? WHERE THE HELL IS THAT?

IT'S HERE. WE'RE HERE.
"OVERLIJDEN"

IT'S COLD. I DON'T WANT TO BE HERE.

WELL, WE HAVE TO FIND A DOCTOR...
UGCH.

THERE'S JOCKS EVERYWHERE.
AND CREEPY GUYS IN LEATHER JACKETS.

I WANT FOOD. I NEED FOOD. I'M FUCKING COLD!
YOU NEED TO BUY A SMARTPHONE.

YOU NEED TO BUY A FUCKING SMARTPHONE!
AND I DON'T KNOW WHERE TO EAT...

DO YOU WANT TO GO TO A RESTAURANT OR A CAFE OR~

ARGH! NOWHERE FANCY! NO VEGETABLES!

bile
McDONALDS 24hr

...I'M HAVING A HORRIBLE TIME...

SO, UH...

I'VE GOT A LOT OF STUFF TO GET ON WITH...

DO YOU THINK MAYBE YOU'LL BE OFF SOON?

... AND I KIND OF NEED MY COMPUTER...

BUT I...
I DON'T HAVE ANYWHERE ELSE TO GO...

YOU REALLY CAN'T STAY WITH MIKE?

NO. I TOLD YOU. HE'S MAD ABOUT THE HERPES I GAVE HIM.

WHAT ABOUT BOOGER?

I GAVE BOOGER HERPES TOO.
AT THE SAME PARTY.

AND YOUR WIFE?

HERPES. AND GONORREAH.
... AND I MADE OUT WITH HER SISTER AT THE DOG TRACK. OKAY: I FUCKED HER.

JESUS CHRIST.

SHE'S TRYING TO TAKE THE KIDS AWAY FROM ME!
LITTLE DIESEL AND JAXON!

WHAT ARE THEY GONNA DO WITHOUT THEIR PAPA-DOODLE?!
...

...

OH, MAN. I GOTTA PISS.
UGH. CAN YOU PLEASE USE THE TOILET?

NAH, I'M FINE. I'LL JUST USE MY PISS-WINDOW...

OH, GOD!
"RELATIONSHIPS"!!!

FUCK! SUSAN, I'M SORRY!

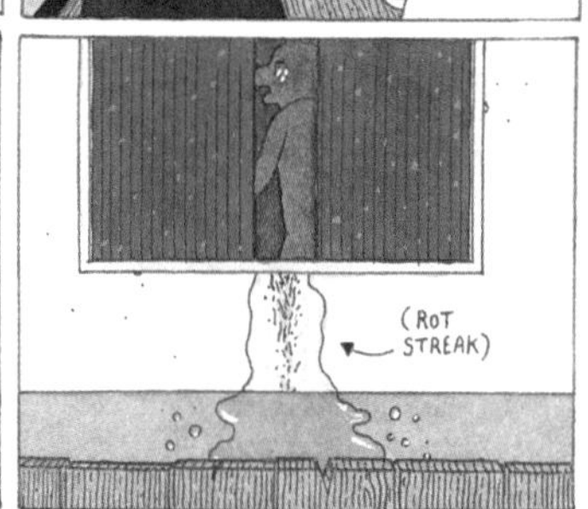
(ROT STREAK)

AND I'VE STILL GOT FEELINGS FOR MEGG!
GODDAMMIT, I'M IN LOVE WITH HER, OWL!

FUCK...

I HAVE FEELINGS FOR YOU TOO...

I, I...

WELCOME, FOLKS, TO FLIGHT VC22 DIRECT TO AMSTERDAM.
EAT PRAY LOVE

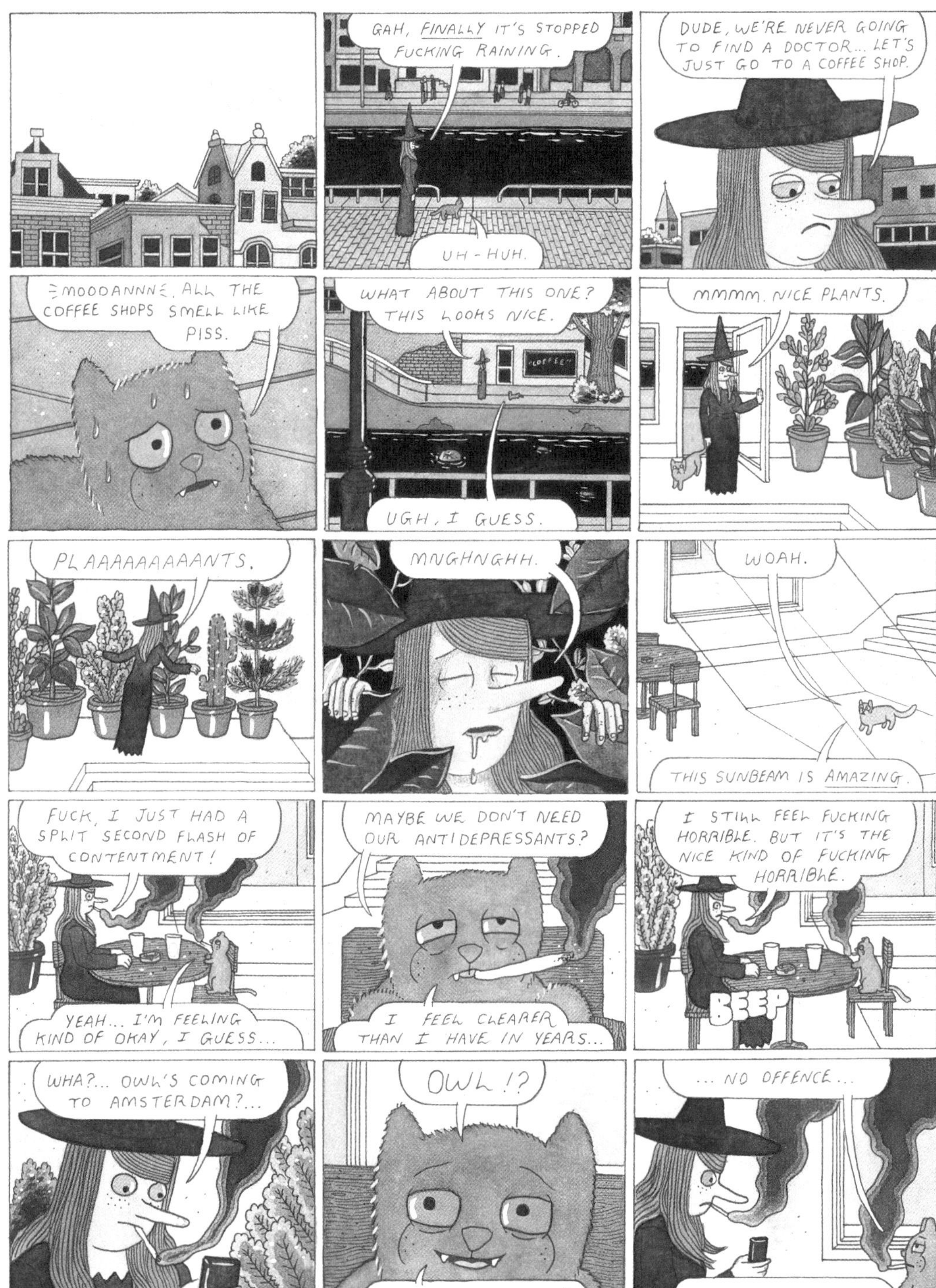
GAH, FINALLY IT'S STOPPED FUCKING RAINING.
UH-HUH.
DUDE, WE'RE NEVER GOING TO FIND A DOCTOR... LET'S JUST GO TO A COFFEE SHOP.
≡MOODANNN≡. ALL THE COFFEE SHOPS SMELL LIKE PISS.
WHAT ABOUT THIS ONE? THIS LOOKS NICE.
"COFFEE"
UGH, I GUESS.
MMMM. NICE PLANTS.
PLAAAAAAAAANTS.
MNGHNGHH.
WOAH.
THIS SUNBEAM IS AMAZING.
FUCK, I JUST HAD A SPLIT SECOND FLASH OF CONTENTMENT!
YEAH... I'M FEELING KIND OF OKAY, I GUESS...
MAYBE WE DON'T NEED OUR ANTIDEPRESSANTS?
I FEEL CLEARER THAN I HAVE IN YEARS...
I STILL FEEL FUCKING HORRIBLE. BUT IT'S THE NICE KIND OF FUCKING HORRIBLE.
BEEP
WHA?... OWL'S COMING TO AMSTERDAM?...
OWL!?
OH, THANK GOD!
... NO OFFENCE...
BUT THANK GOD.

OH MY GOD! THERE HE IS!
HEY GUYS.
OWL!

WE'RE SO HAPPY TO SEE YOU!
... REALLY?

WE MISSED YOU SO MUCH!!

AWW, THAT'S SO SWEET...
OH HEY, YOU GUYS FORGOT YOUR PILLS!

LET ME JUST-
WAIT A MINUTE

WHAT THE?
HAHAHAHAHAHA!

NICE GLASS DILDOS, OWL.
HAHAHAHA!

THIS- THIS ISN'T MY SUITCASE...

HAHAHA, SUUUUUURE IT ISN'T.

JESUS CHRIST, OWL! YOU'RE A FUCKING MANIAC!
YOU'RE INSATIABLE!

THEY'RE NOT MINE!
I DON'T EVEN HAVE A DILDO!

... THAT'S NOT WHAT I'VE HEARD...

HE!

DAT IS VERDOMME MIJN HOFFER!

... GEBROKEN!

IT WASN'T ME! I DIDN'T BREAK THEM!

JE BETAALT VOOR DEZE, U STUK STRONT!

HOE VIND JE HET LEUK ALS IK BREEK JE SPULLEN?!

MY CASE!
NO!!

CRASH!

FUCK U.
IDIOOT BUITENLANDER!

...

FUCK.
MY AFTERSHAVE...

AHA!
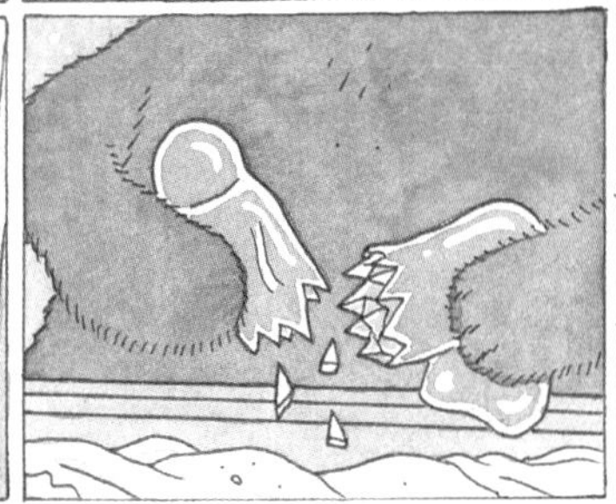

I KNEW IT.
...

"COFFEE" SHOP

YOU'RE NOT SMOKING, OWL?

UH, NO... I'M GOING TO WAIT UNTIL AFTER.
...

SO YOU GUYS ARE OFF YOUR PILLS?
UH-HUH.

FUCK THAT CORPORATE BULLSHIT.

INTO THE FUCKING RIVER.

OOH, WE'RE HERE!

THE ANNE FRANK HOUSE!
WOW! AMAZING.

UGCH. THAT LINE IS HUUUUUUGE.

OH, GOD. THIS IS GOING TO TAKE FOREVER.

... HERE WE GO.
OOH!
LIGHT

SERIOUSLY? GUYS, THAT IS COMPLETELY TASTELESS.

THIS IS THE ANNE FRANK HOUSE.
DO YOU REALLY NEED TO BE THAT HIGH?

BLECH. IT'S JUST A DEPRESSING OLD WAR-HOUSE...
THIS IS SHIT, OWL.

BYE.
WE'RE GOING TO THE RED LIGHT DISTRICT.

... GUYS! STOP RUNNING!
... WAIT UP!!

... WOAH...
PUFF

WOAH...

TEEHEEHEEHEE

WOAH! LOOK AT THE BUTTHOLE ON HER!
HOLY FUCK!

OH MY GOD!
GASP!

...
UGH.

THIS IS ACTUALLY KIND OF GROSS...

OOH, LET'S GO TO THE RIJKSMUSEUM!
HMMM... OKAY.

RIGHT. LET'S DO IT...
HAHAHAHAHAHAHAHA.

MNGH.
HAHAHA!

WAIT... WHAT'S THE...?
HAHAHAHAHAHAHA

HELLO.
ARE YOU OKAY...?

... DO YOU KNOW WHERE YOU ARE?
BUH.

. . .

FUCK THIS.

CRACK

HMMMMM...

... I GUESS OWL
TOOK HIS DILDO...

SIGH

LOOK, I'M SHORRY.

I SHOULD HAVE TOLD YOU BOTH...

I FUCKED UP.
I'M MAN ENOUGH TO ADMIT IT.

CAN'T WE JUSHT FORGET THIS SHIT?

I DON'T WANT TO DO THIS LOVER'S TIFF ROUTINE...

LETSH JUSHT FUCK.
WE'VE ALL GOT MY HERPES NOW... WHAT DOESH IT MATTER?

...ZZZZZ

WOOMF

WOOOOOOOOOO!
HAHAHAHA!
B'OH!
SIP
HAHAHAHAHAHA
CRASH
HEY!
HAHAHAHAHAHAHA
CRASH
GUYS, STOP IT!
FUCK OFF, MOGG!
YOU'RE RUNNING ME OFF THE ROAD!
HAHAHA HAHA!
GODDAMMIT!
HAHAHAHAHA!
ARGH, STAY AWAY FROM ME!
FUCK!
HAHAHAHAHA!
GAH... OUCH!
YOU GUYS ARE ACTING FUCKED.
ARE YOU FEELING OKAY?
ARGH!
BREAK

COFFEE SHOP

... OF COURSE THE INDIVIDUAL NATIONS COULD STILL HAVE LIMITED TREASURIES LIKE THE STATES.

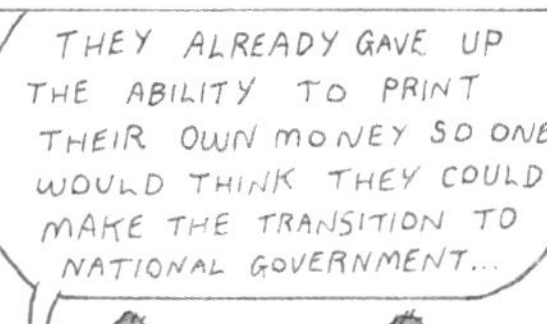
THEY ALREADY GAVE UP THE ABILITY TO PRINT THEIR OWN MONEY SO ONE WOULD THINK THEY COULD MAKE THE TRANSITION TO NATIONAL GOVERNMENT...

UH-HUH.

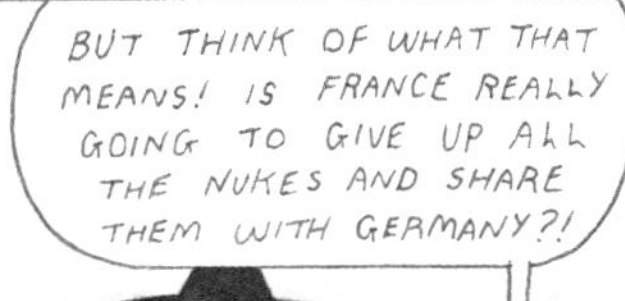
BUT THINK OF WHAT THAT MEANS! IS FRANCE REALLY GOING TO GIVE UP ALL THE NUKES AND SHARE THEM WITH GERMANY?!

ARE THE PIIGS GOING TO TRUST THAT ALLIANCE OF GERMANY & FRANCE?

SIP

I CAN TELL YOU THIS: THE BRITISH ARE THANKING THEIR LUCKY STARS THAT THEY DON'T HAVE TO SHARE THEIR NUKES WITH GERMANY!

NO STINKING EURO FOR THEM!

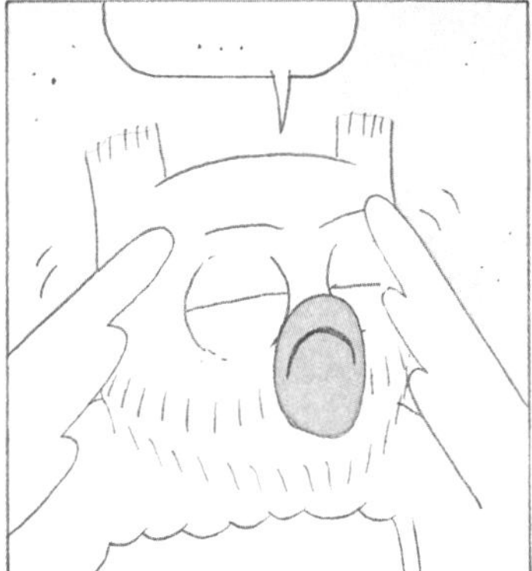
...

ARE YOU OKAY, MEGG?

... YEAH... I'M... FINE...

...

SO. WHAT ARE WE DOING?

YOU GUYS DON'T SEEM TO WANT TO DO ANY-THING I WANT TO DO.

MOGG, YOU HAVE YET TO APOLOGIZE FOR BREAKING MY LEG...

OWL, I'M FLIPPING OUT... THE - THE MIRROR...
... I'M FREAKING ME OUT.

FOR FUCK'S SAKE, MEGG, JUST LOOK SOMEWHERE ELSE THEN!
SNAP

...

GAAAAAAARBAGE.
FUCKING SLAG.

MNGHH.
MEGG?
WHERE ARE YOU GOING?

I'M TOO AWARE OF MYSELF!

FUCK. MOGG, LET'S MOVE.
SHIT.

... I BELIEVE, OWL, THAT THE SOVEREIGN MELD IS A BIG LIE.
GODDAMMIT, WHERE DID SHE GO?!

THE NATIONS WITHIN THE EUROZONE ARE STILL FIERCELY INDEPENDENT!

3 HOURS LATER:
... BUT THE ISSUE IS THE UNION! IT'S TH-
OH MY GOD, MEGG!

HEY, BOYS, YOOOO HOOOOOO!
WHAT ARE YOU DOING, MEGG?!

I CAME BACK AND FOUND OUR PILLS AND I TOOK ALL THE PILLS...

COME ON IN, THE WATER'S DELICIOUS!
I'M A BEAUTIFUL SWAN!

I'M PUNCHING HOLES IN BOATS...
WOOOO!

...

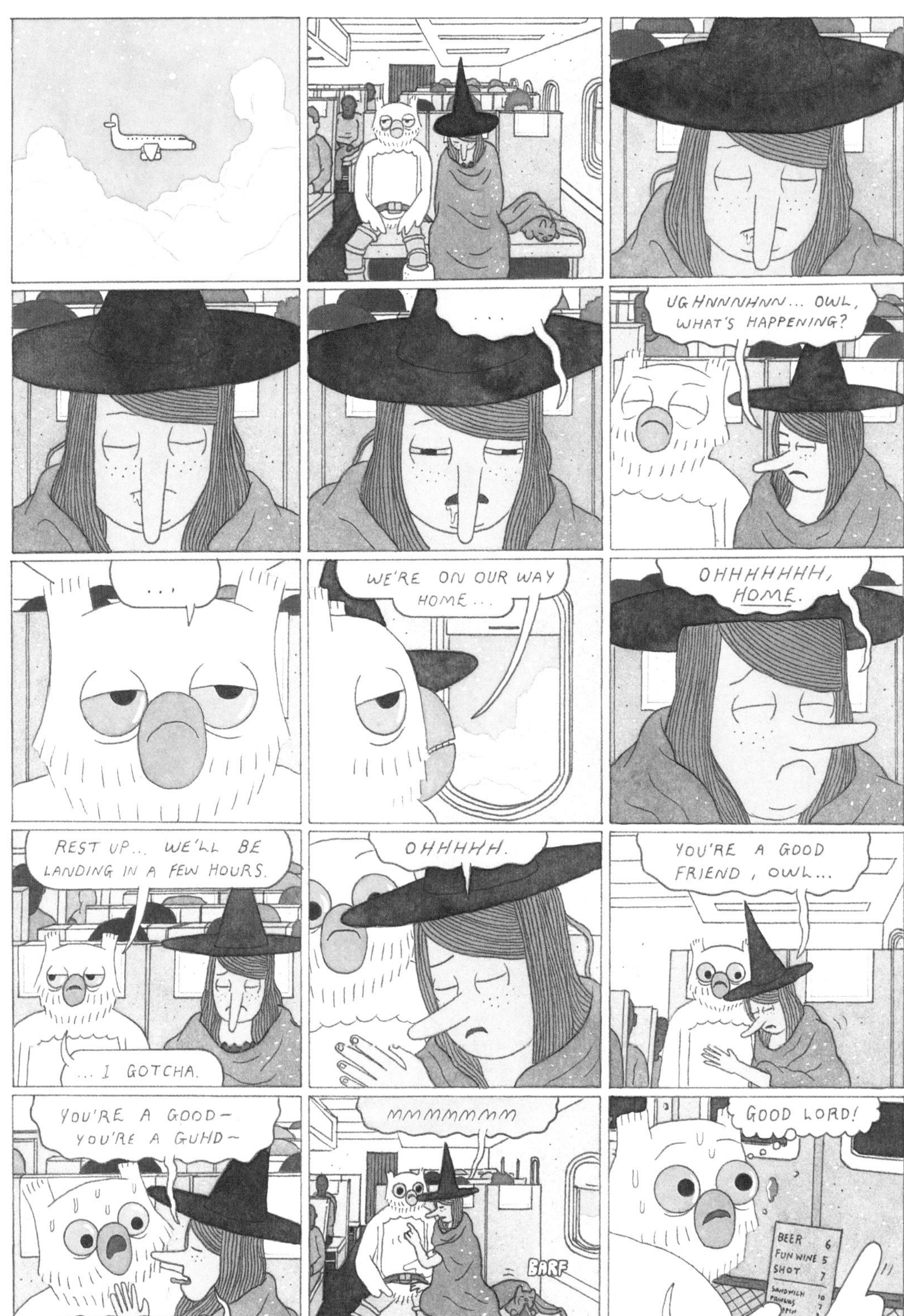
...
UGHNNNHNN... OWL, WHAT'S HAPPENING?
...
WE'RE ON OUR WAY HOME...
OHHHHHHH, HOME.
REST UP... WE'LL BE LANDING IN A FEW HOURS.
... I GOTCHA.
OHHHHH.
YOU'RE A GOOD FRIEND, OWL...
YOU'RE A GOOD-
YOU'RE A GUHD-
YEYHR GH...
MMMMMMMM
BARF
GOOD LORD!
BEER 6
FUN WINE 5
SHOT 7
... EXCUSE ME, HOSTESS!

YOU OKAY? YOU ALRIGHT?
YEAH... WE'RE OKAY.
WHAT THE FUCK?!
WHY IS THE FRONT DOOR OPEN?!
WAIT THERE, MEGG...
PEEP
I'LL CHECK THIS OUT...
"FUCK ZONE"?...
FUCK ZONE
WEREWOLF JONES!!
OH, HEY, OWL.
WHAT'S UP?
HEY. I'M DRACULA JUNIOR.
WHA! - WHA! -
WHAT THE FUCK, WEREWOLF JONES?!
"FUCK ZONE"?!
PSST. HEY, WW...
THERE ANY EXTRA LUBE AROUND?
CHECK OWL'S ROOM.
NAH, MAN. IT'S TAPPED.
... SHIT.
OH MY GOD!!
THIS IS UNACCEPTABLE! THIS IS UNACCEPTABLE!!
ALRIGHT, ALRIGHT. CALM DOWN, JIMMY CORRIGAN.
LET ME FINISH MY B.J.

WHAT'S GOING ON?...

MEGG!

OH, GOOD TO SEE YOU, WEREWOLF JONES.
HOW ARE YOU?

AH, NOT SO GREAT...
Y'KNOW?

YEAH...
I KNOW.

OOH, LET'S WATCH SOME JUDGE JUDY!
CLICK

NO!
CLICK
NO JUDGE JUDY!

I HAVE HALF A MIND TO CALL THE POLICE, WEREWOLF JONES.

YOU CANNOT DO THIS!

THIS IS NOT COOL!

OH, C'MON MAN. I'LL CLEAN UP.

WHAT'S THE FUCKING PROBLEM?
OOH!

YEAH, SIT DOWN, OWL. WE'VE HAD A LONG TRIP.

AND IT'S JUST SO NICE TO BE HOME.
SPIT

TWITCH

YEAH AND I'VE BEEN DOING IT TOUGH, OWL!
I GOT BURNT UP REAL BAD!
OH, POOR WW!
UH-HUH.
I'M ASSUMING THAT EX-PLAINS THIS HUGE BURN MARK ON THE CARPET.
OH, WHO CARES ABOUT THE STUPID CARPET, OWL!
ARE YOU OKAY, WW?
I'M SURVIVING, MEGG...
ONE DAY AT A TIME...
BUT I COULD REALLY USE SOME HUGS RIGHT NOW.
GET ON IN HERE!
GOOD TO SEE YOU, FRIENDS.
YOU TOO.
HEY, UH... YOU DON'T HAVE ANY LUBE ON YOU DO YOU?
NO I DO NOT.
...
YEAH YOU DO, OWL...
I SAW IT IN YOUR SUITCASE.
SERIOUSLY?...
PFF. DICKHEAD.

ALRIGHT, THAT'S IT! OUT!

EVERYBODY OUT!
ZIP

THIS IS OVER!
NO MORE "FUCK ZONE"!

OVER!

FINE, BAH.
SEE YOU LATER, WEREWOLF JONES.

=SIGH= BYE, GUYS...

YOU TOO, WW!
OUT!

DUDE... I HAVE LITERALLY NOWHERE TO GO.
I PROMISE I'LL CLEAN UP!

I DIDN'T KNOW YOU'D BE BACK SO SOON!

OH, IT WAS AWFUL, WW!
I'M NEVER LEAVING THE HOUSE EVER AGAIN!

COME ON, OWL.
WW CAN SLEEP IN THE SHED.

YEAH, COME ON, OWL.
SHUT THE FUCK UP AND GIVE WW A HUG.

C'MON...
♫ GIMME A HUUUUUUG ♫
C'MOOOOOOON.

EVERYTHING WILL GET CLEANED UP GOOD AS NEW.

GIMME A HUG.

UGH.

THERE YOU GO!
SPIN
OH YEAH!

YAAAAAY!

...

GOOSE

ARGH!!

WHAT THE FUCK?!
UGCH!

OH, YEAH, I GOT CUSTODY OF THE BOYS AGAIN. THAT COOL?
YEAH, WHATEVER.

Marriott
DING

. . .
BUSINESS CENTRE
Gmail
BACCO
PAPAJOHN's
NAILS
SEXY LAND
DILDOS, VIDEOS, LINGERIE, ACCESSORIES, DOL
BEEP
. . .
WHA? WHAT THE FUCK?!
FLUSH
ZIP
OH, HEY, OWL.

WHAT THE HELL ARE YOU DOING HERE, WEREWOLF JONES?!

HOW ON EARTH DID YOU EVEN FIND ME?!
HOW DID YOU GET IN HERE?!

OH MY GOD! PLEASE CLOSE THAT DOOR!
WHAT HAVE YOU BEEN EATING?

UGH.

SLOW DOWN WITH THE QUESTIONS...

I FIGURED I'D GIVE MEGG AND MOGG SOME SPACE...

UGCH, CAN YOU PLEASE NOT PUT YOUR ASS ALL OVER MY PILLOWS?

WHAT?
ARE YOU SERIOUS?

OH, JESUS CHRIST.

TOSS

THERE! HAPPY?

...
WELL, NO, FRANKLY!

I'M HUNGRY, DADDY...
MMM, ME TOO, BOYS...

DO YOU THINK WE COULD PINCH A FEW SLICES, OWL?

NO!
NO, YOU MAY NOT!

GET THE FUCK OUT OF HERE!!

LEAVE ME THE HELL ALONE!!

...

MY GOD, YOU ARE SO FUCKING SELFISH, OWL!

YOU DON'T GIVE A FUCK ABOUT ANY OF US DO YOU?!

EVERYTHING'S ALWAYS GOT TO BE OWL'S WAY!

...GET YOUR FILTHY FUCKING PAW OUT OF MY FACE. NOW.

WHATEVER. FUCK YOU!

I FIGURED I'D BE NICE AND GIVE MEGG & MOGG SOME COUPLE TIME...

IT'S FUCKING TOUGH BEING IN A RELATION-SHIP!
I GUESS YOU WOULDN'T KNOW.

NOBODY CAN PUT UP WITH YOUR CONTROLLING, PEDANTIC BULLSHIT!

C'MON BOYS, LET'S GO.
UNCLE OWL NEEDS TO JERK OFF HIS TINY DICK.

SERIOUSLY, OWL.
FUCK. YOU.

SLAM

ARGH!
FUCK YOU!

FUCKING WEREWOLF JONES!!

HEY?!
MY PIZZA! MY STUFF!

HAHAHAHAHAAHAHA!

MMMMM!
HAHAHAHAHAHA!

WHAT ELSE DO WE HAVE HERE?

STRAWBERRY LUBE...

PETITE PRINCESS PLUG.
MMMM, NICE WEIGHT.

LINGERIE WITCHES DVD...
HOT

VIBRATING COCK RING.

WOAH, DIESEL, DON'T EAT THAT.
THAT'S NOT CANDY.

WHA?...

IT'S NOT CANDY. IT'S SPECIAL GREASE. FOR YOUR BOTTOM.
?
FOR ADULT'S BOTTOMS.

C'MON, LET'S GO. DADDY NEEDS TO GET TO THE PAWN SHOP.

"COUPLES TIME"

MMM.

DO UH...
DO YOU WANNA FUCK?

EW, NO, GET OFF ME.

HEY, YOU WERE HOLDING ME.

I DIDN'T WANT TO SIT ON YOUR BONY LEGS...

I WANT TO SPRAWL AROUND ON MY SPOT.

FINE.

WHAT EVER.

C'MOOOOOOOON.
PAWN
WE BUY PORN

LOOK THIS FUCKER UP ONLINE.

THIS IS A QUALITY PLUG.

GOLD PLATED.

I WANT 40 FOR IT.

I'LL GIVE YOU 30.
BOO YAH!

OHHHHHH YEEAHHHH.

HAHAHAHAHA.
STUPID OWL.

OWL IS A CUNT.
I HATE HIM.

"I WISH HE WAS LYING IN A DITCH WITH A SLIT THROAT AND A LOAD IN HIS ASS"

DIESEL!?...
THAT'S A BIT HARSH.

YOU SAID THAT, DADDY.
I DID?...

FUCK.

BOYS, OWL ISN'T SO BAD... HE'S JUST A BIT OF AN ASSHOLE NARC...

...
I'M HAVING A RARE MOMENT OF EMPATHY, BOYS...

C'MON, LET'S GO!
?

BACK TO THE MARRIOT!
...

BANG BANG BANG BANG

OWL!
OOOOOWL!

OPEN UP!

NO!
GET OUT OF HERE!

LEAVE ME ALONE!

BANG BANG BANG BANG BANG BANG

FUCK OFF!!
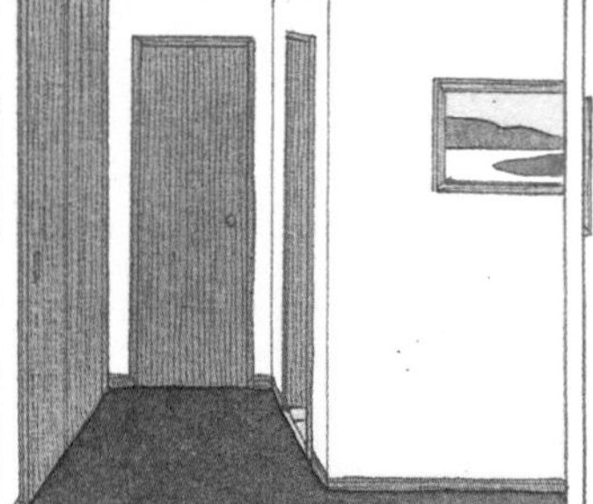

CRASH!

I'M SORRY, OWL!
I'M SORRY!

I'VE BEEN DISRESPECTFUL!
I KNOW THAT!

LOOK! I GOT YOU THIS FROZEN PIZZA!
PAPA BUDGETS

DIESEL WANTS YOU TO HAVE THESE FLOWERS.

AND JAXON'S GOT A CUCUMBER FOR YOU TO STICK IN YOUR BUM.

I WANNA MAKE AMENDS!

I NEED YOU GUYS IN MY LIFE!

YOU'RE A GOOD GUY, OWL!
YOU'RE A POSITIVE INFLUENCE!

...I'M TRYING TO BE THE BIGGER MAN HERE, OWL.

I'M SORRY!
I WANNA FIX THINGS!

...

AV
AV
AV
. .
WELL WHAT THE FUCK DO YOU WANNA DO THEN?

WHAT'S GOING ON? ARE WE BREAKING UP?
DO YOU WANT TIME APART?
...
KINDA... YEAH.
BUT I DON'T WANT TO LEAVE THE HOUSE...
AND YOU NEVER LEAVE THE HOUSE.
BUT YEAH... I THINK I NEED SOME TIME ALONE TO FIGURE SHIT OUT
GREAT. AWESOME.
FUCK.
GOD, FUCK YOU.
WHERE THE FUCK AM I SUPPOSED TO GO?!
I DON'T KNOW!

I'M JUST SICK OF YOUR FUCKING FACE IN MY SHIT EVERY-DAY...
SIGH
FUCK.
FUCK.
RAGHH!

IS THIS BETTER?!
...
I'LL JUST WEAR A MASK NOW.
THIS IS ME NOW.
OKAY.
THAT ACTUALLY DOES MAKE A DIFFERENCE.

FUCK.
WHAT ARE WE GOING TO DO?

I'M GOING BACK ONTO THE PILLS.

I'M PROBABLY GOING TO KILL MYSELF IF I DON'T.
I CAN'T BE CLEAR LIKE THIS...
I NEED TO FOG MYSELF UP.

NO! DON'T GO ON THE PILLS!

I THINK WE'RE LEVELING OUT AGAIN!

SIGH

HEY, GUYS!

HOW ARE YOU?
ARE YOU GUYS OKAY?

HEY, HEY, NONE OF THAT!

OWL, GET MEGG A COCKTAIL.
ON IT.

WHITE RUSSIAN?

O-OKAY...
YEAH...

I'VE BOUGHT SOME PAINT WITH MY BUTT PLUG MONEY.
LET'S GET THIS PLACE ALL NICE AGAIN!

WE'RE A FAMILY!

WE'RE AT OUR BEST TOGETHER!

PAPA DOODLE'S GONNA TAKE CARE OF EVERYTHING!

HERE YOU GO, MEGG.
THANK YOU...

SIP

WW, WHERE ARE DIESEL AND JAXON?

OH, I SENT THEM OFF TO BEG AT THE DUMP.

I'M GONNA PAY YOU BACK, MAN!
SERIOUSLY, I'M ON TOP OF ALL THIS SHIT.

SOMETHING HAPPENED AFTER I PAWNED THAT BUTT PLUG...
IT WAS A BEAUTIFUL MOMENT.

EVERYTHING'S GOING TO BE FINE, MEGG!

CREDITS:
WRITTEN AND DRAWN BY SIMON HANSELMANN
2010-2015. RICHMOND UPON THAMES, LONDON.
EAGLEMONT, VICTORIA. BRUNSWICK EAST, VICTORIA.
SEATTLE, WASHINGTON. VARIOUS AIRPORTS.
JUNIOR STAFF WRITER/PERSONAL ASSISTANT: HTML FLOWERS.
THANK YOU: JACQ COHEN
HTML FLOWERS
ALESSANDRA STERNFELD
ERIC REYNOLDS
PAUL BARESH
GARY GROTH
KAREN CONRAD
NICK GAZIN
JASON LEIVIAN
MICHAEL RENAUD
RONNIE SCOTT
MICHAEL FIKARIS
JMKE
WARD ZWART
BOOGER BRIE
JESSICA CIOCCI
BERLIAC
FRANK SANTORO
PIGEON BOYS
MISMA EDITIONS
КОМИЛЬФО
REY NARANJO
FULGENCIO PIMENTEL
BREAKDOWN PRESS
YOU
OTHER MEGG, MOGG AND OWL PUBLICATIONS:
MEGAHEX (FANTAGRAPHICS)
WORST BEHAVIOUR (PIGEON PRESS)
LIFE ZONE (SPACE FACE BOOKS)
FORTHCOMING:
BAD GATEWAY
MEGG'S COVEN
WEBSITES TO VISIT:
GIRLMOUNTAIN.TUMBLR.COM
INSTAGRAM: @SIMON.HANSELMANN
WWW.FANTAGRAPHICS.COM
"PORTIONS OF THIS WORK PREVIOUSLY APPEARED":
ON VICE.COM
AS A BROADSHEET NEWSPAPER PUBLISHED BY FLOATING WORLD, PORTLAND.
BONUS INSERT IN "ST. OWL'S BAY ARTIST EDITION".
IN THE LIFTED BROW.
IN THE PITCHFORK REVIEW.
IN INFINITE WALKTHROUGH (ZINE WITH HTML FLOWERS AND JMKE) (SELF PUBLISHED).
IN WEREWOLF JONES & SONS ISSUE ONE (WRITTEN WITH HTML FLOWERS. SELF PUBLISHED.)
SELF PUBLISHED MM&O ZINE, 2010.
RISOGRAPHED BOOKLET PUBLISHED BY SILENT ARMY TO ACCOMPANY A WEED GRINDER.
ЛУЧШЕ ВСЕХ. THE RUSSIAN EDITION OF MM&O. PUBLISHED BY КОМИЛЬФО, ST. PETERSBERG.
IN SANS SOLEIL 2. ZINE BY WARD ZWART.
IN MAGICA BLANCA, IN SPANISH, PUBLISHED BY REY NARANJO, COLOMBIA.
"ON THE INTERNET".
FANTAGRAPHICS BOOKS

SIMON HANSELMANN WAS BORN IN 1981
IN LAUNCESTON, TASMANIA. HE HAS
WORKED AS A FRY COOK, AS A SCRUBBER
OF BIRD SHIT, AND NOW AS A CARTOONIST.
HE CURRENTLY LIVES IN SEATTLE, WASH-
INGTON WITH HIS WIFE, A ONE-EYED
DOG AND A GANG OF WHITE RABBITS.